SCRIPT TEASE

SCRIPT TEASE

A WORDSMITH'S WAXINGS ON LIFE AND WRITING

ERIC NICOL

Illustrations by Dave More

DUNDURN PRESS
TORONTO

Project Editor: Michael Carroll
Copy Editor: Nicole Chaplin
Design: Courtney Horner
Printer: Webcom

Library and Archives Canada Cataloguing in Publication

Nicol, Eric, 1919-
       Script tease : a wordsmith's waxings on life
and writing / by Eric Nicol.

ISBN 978-1-55488-707-1

       1. Nicol, Eric, 1919- --Humour.
2. Writing--Humour. I. Title.

PS8527.I35S37 2010   C818'.5402   C2009-907467-2

1 2 3 4 5   14 13 12 11 10

Conseil des Arts
du Canada

Canada Council
for the Arts

Canadä

ONTARIO ARTS COUNCIL
CONSEIL DES ARTS DE L'ONTARIO

We acknowledge the support of the **Canada Council for the Arts** and the **Ontario Arts Council** for our publishing program. We also acknowledge the financial support of the **Government of Canada** through the **Canada Book Fund** and **The Association for the Export of Canadian Books**, and the **Government of Ontario** through the **Ontario Book Publishers Tax Credit program**, and the **Ontario Media Development Corporation**.

Care has been taken to trace the ownership of copyright material used in this book. The author and the publisher welcome any information enabling them to rectify any references or credits in subsequent editions.

J. Kirk Howard, President

Printed and bound in Canada.
Printed on recycled paper.

www.dundurn.com

Dundurn Press	Gazelle Book Services Limited	Dundurn Press
3 Church Street, Suite 500	White Cross Mills	2250 Military Road
Toronto, Ontario, Canada	High Town, Lancaster, England	Tonawanda, NY
M5E 1M2	LA1 4XS	U.S.A. 14150

To my wife, Mary Razzell, my compassionate editor

CONTENTS

THE WRITE STUFF:
AN AUTHOR'S HANDBOOK

A WORDSMITH'S WAXINGS

THE WRITE STUFF:
AN AUTHOR'S HANDBOOK

SALUTATION

Welcome, class, to this first lecture in Creative Writing 100, Creative Writing 200, 300, and time permitting, Creative Writing 100 repeated!

The beauty of these printed lectures is that if you need to go to the bathroom, you don't have to raise your hand. You may certainly hold up your hand if you wish to relieve tension or exhibit a manicure without risk of drawing extra homework. But what you do in the privacy of your own home, or indeed anyone else's home, won't affect your grade, particularly as you won't be given a grade unless you pay an additional fee on completion of the course.

First, though, what *is* creative writing? How do you distinguish it from, say, your grocery shopping list? The answer is you *can't*. In fact, your first assignment in this course will be to turn in a creative grocery shopping list that reveals shades of character, as well as some truly deplorable eating habits.

Second, you need to distinguish between *creativity* and *creationism*.

Creationism is the belief in Adam and Eve and going to hell with Charles Darwin. But *creativity* derives from a creator who doesn't believe in the apple except as a brand of computer.

Third, creative writing is the second-most satisfying thing you can do lying down. In fact, creative writing *is* like sex, it being a mental orgasm that is passionate even though the result is stillborn.

This doesn't mean you can ignore your physical condition, assuming your Muse is also overweight. Actually, this course requires you to do twenty push-ups before every lecture. Why? Because publishers won't even consider your work unless you are in good enough shape to survive the *book promotion tour*. Some publishers now require that your manuscript be accompanied by a complete medical report, signed by three different doctors, along with a recent photo of the author holding up his chin without undue effort.

This explains why poets like Lord Byron (bad leg) and John Milton (clinically blind) could never get published today. Oscar Wilde might encounter less of the trouble he bought as a gay wit, but he would balk at having to get up at five in the morning in a strange town to appear on a radio talk show hosted by a sadist who secretly hates books.

Yes, it does help if you own your own aircraft, but not much.

Now, besides having it in the legs, how strong is your *motivation*?

Have you defined in your own mind if you are too shy to talk about *why* you want to engage in creative writing? If it's just because you think you look more meaningful in a houndstooth jacket or shapeless sweater, or it's against your religion to engage in more lucrative work, your motivation may lack substance.

Here is the key: it's not enough to *want* to write. You must *need* to write as a supplement to breathing. You should see writer's block as the worst kind of constipation.

The valid writer is *possessed* by writing. Of all his possessions, this will probably prove to be the least valuable. No matter. It's a must.

When the Muse orders "Jump!" You just say "How high?"

Never mind about cheating on your spouse or tax return; when you really need to feel guilty is when you have done no writing in the day.

This is why, of all the natural disasters the world assaults us with, none is as cataclysmic as the computer crash. Or a pencil sharpener refusing to have intercourse.

Such frustration is particularly traumatic for the female author for whom writing is surrogate motherhood. The book has a gestation period comparable to that of an ordinary baby. Both, at birth, are put in a wrapper and displayed fondly to the public. And instead of reading *to* her child, she reads *from* it to her creative-writing class, or any other living object with ears to hear.

TOOLING UP

B esides divine afflatus, what other gear do you need in order to become the next Margaret Atwood or Stephen King or even the author of a raging letter to the editor of the publication that rejected your poem?

First, you need to have access to a word processor. Is it realistic to hope that you can process your words yourself, with God's guidance or a helpful secretary who really needs the money? Alas, no way. The ugly fact is that to be a writer today you must have a meaningful relationship with a *computer*. Nobody knows how William Shakespeare was able to get along without it and still have a sex life. Apparently, he had to write everything in *longhand*.

I sense eyebrows being raised. Well, class, longhand is, or was, a form of *handwriting*. Handwriting is what you do if you endorse a cheque. Still unclear? Then let's just say that writing longhand not only takes more time than typing but reveals more about the writer's own character than a graphologist would feel comfortable reporting.

The hazard of handwriting was first recognized by Omar Khayyám:

> The Moving Finger writes; and having writ,
> Moves on: nor all thy Piety nor Wit
> Shall lure it back to cancel half a Line,
> Nor all thy Tears wash out a Word of it.

Why? Because Omar *couldn't use the delete key!* He may not have even owned a computer. If he didn't, it was surely false economy. That's why all members of this class are urged to make whatever sacrifice of lifestyle — food, drink, clothes, child support, cheesecake — necessary for you to be able to afford to buy this *sine qua non*: the PC.

And a *printer*. (Why should we deny ourselves the thrill of seeing our work in print, just because it's not yet ready?)

Note: self-publication will be dealt with, severely, in a later section.

If your computer is indisposed, it is normal to make a rough copy in *pencil*. For those of you unfamiliar with this writing instrument: a pencil is a lead-bearing device normally held between the fingers when not being chewed during creative ecstasy. The tip of the pencil makes physical contact with paper, creating arousal more sensuous than that provided by the PC.

In moments of divine afflatus, however, the pencil lead may break (*coitus interruptus*). Hence the need for a *pencil sharpener*, a rotary instrument that happily provides relief from the tension of composition, as well as a quantity of sawdust that can be used to mulch potted plants.

REFERENCE MATERIAL

It may come as a shock to the novice writer to learn that his computer doesn't know everything. Even that god almighty, the Internet, may lack verbal skills acquired only by *Webster* or *Oxford*. Yes, you need a *dictionary*. If you have no other book on your shelf, this is the first to replace the framed photo of your lover. Your computer may catch misspellings, regardless of whether you want it to or not, but is hapless when it comes to the shades of meaning you need to set your work apart from an ordinary ferry schedule.

There is a world of difference between *denotation* and *connotation*, and you will need a dictionary to find out what it is. Other vital material:

1. *Bartlett's Familiar Quotations*. If you suspect that you aren't the first playwright to pen "To be, or not to be, that is the question," *Bartlett* will confirm your suspicion and identify the author who took the unfair advantage of being anterior.

2. *Roget's Thesaurus*. A cornucopia of synonyms. Essential for the writer searching for *le mot juste* (i.e., a French phrase that sounds sexy). Very often the word you want is on the tip of your tongue but won't get off. In the course of writing a long work, words can build up on the tip of your tongue, creating a condition called *lingual overload*. The remedy, too often, is alcohol administered internally. Better far to be able to resort to your thesaurus where you will find so many engaging synonyms that you may just abandon your novel to concentrate on crossword puzzles.

3. *Fowler's Modern English Usage*. Fowler, who seems to have had no first name but overcame this handicap with typical British pluck, is to writing style what Alfred Kinsey is to sexual intercourse. He had very strong views about the conjunctive. As for italics, which imply emotional gestures and involuntary lip movement, his reservations are to be respected even as they are widely ignored by twenty-first-century authors. In short, for safer intercourse with the Muse, every writer should have a *Fowler* on his bookshelf, if only for its benign censure.

THE WRITER'S IMAGE

Now, class, I suspect that some of you are quite well dressed.

That has got to stop.

Granted, once you commit to writing for a living, your stylish dressing will cease automatically. Sartorially speaking, you can't start projecting an image of an unmade bed too soon. Your uncoordinated garments reflect your total concentration on your writing, on your garbing a sentence with an appropriate adverb, or choosing the right simile to set off a verbal ensemble.

Your visual effect should be that of a university professor who has gained tenure and can limit his dress standards to checking his zipper.

Does this mean smoking a pipe? As long as there is no tobacco in the pipe, this can be a useful prop, especially for the female author. A cigar? Never. Virginia Woolf was said to have been seen going for long walks smoking a meerschaum, but only she would have been neurotic enough to carry that off.

Now, what about the appropriate underwear for the beginning author? Not Calvin Klein, obviously. The mind boggles at the concept of Bernard Shaw wearing a thong. Putting on worldly skivvies is a bad start for the author who wants to bond with the common man, or the even more common woman.

Got a hole in your sock? Congratulations! Your big toe is right there, front if not centre, to remind you that the flesh cannot be denied.

Your fly is open? Your makeup appears to have been applied with a spray gun? Excellent! Further evidence that your full attention is given to your writing, not the trivia of personal appearance.

To sum up: from the top of your bed head to the soles of your grubby sneakers, you the writer should demonstrate your contempt for all outward signs of success. (An unkempt beard is also impressive — especially on the female author.)

Now, this doesn't mandate a total neglect of personal hygiene. Hopefully, there will be occasions — autographing sessions, media interviews — when it is preferable that people can come near you without being overcome by fumes. A hot bath, at least once a month, isn't a philistine luxury; they provide those extra moments of relaxation that generate some of our best ideas, such as topping the bath off with a nap.

THE PHOTO-OP

Now may be the time to have your photo taken … before you're really immersed in rejection slips. When your work *is* accepted by a publisher, the house will want a photo to put on the cover of your book. And you are not going to look any younger before you find a publisher. Appearing haggard or dissipated can be offensive, especially to someone shopping for a children's book.

No, the snapshot that a friend took of you last summer molesting a beach ball may not be suitable if your book is a serious novel. It may be prudent to book a professional photographer who has the skill to personalize the bags under your eyes. It's an expense, true, but tax deductible should your book get published in your lifetime.

Do not get a publicity photo of yourself holding your own chin. Go the whole hog: get a shave. Also, forget the pipe. Even if you actually smoke one, ma'am. And no gazing off toward a brighter horizon. It may have worked for Aldous Huxley, but yours will be a mug shot better suited for the most-wanted list.

Also, remember that studio photo sessions go on for so long, holding rigid body positions, that your eyes — as recorded in the final shot — will show the loss of the will to live. In fact, the only author known to have survived the ordeal without a permanent spastic twitch was Winston Churchill, who had taken the precaution of drinking heavily beforehand. Woody Allen, in *his* studio photos, appears totally suicidal. This is quite fitting, as humour writers (i.e., Robert Benchley, Groucho Marx, George Burns, et al.) have all had the bearing of a Muse that isn't amused.

THE GENDER THING

Okay, now that you've wiped that grin off your face, let's move on to a more serious issue: sex. The question remains: What gender should you be to maximize your chance of success as a creative writer? Male, female or undecided? Don't guess.

At this point in time, fortune appears to favour the female writer, as long as she doesn't overdo it. Exuding her femininity creates the impression that the writer is interested in reproduction of a more bodily nature than that of the Xerox machine.

On the other hand, the female author is much better off today than in the nineteenth century when Mary Ann Evans felt obliged to transmute into George Eliot, and Amandine Aurore Lucie Dupin hit pay dirt only after becoming George Sand.

Today the pendulum has swung the other way. Female authors actually *flaunt* their real names, while the guy named Joe might be tempted to transform into Josephine. This isn't a good way to get in touch with his feminine side.

Most successful novels today are written by gals. Guys feel handicapped. They may even come to resent their own genitalia, as betraying the cause of that creative organ situated above the belt. But this is scapegoating of the worst kind.

Now, if a guy wants to experiment with wearing a bra just to get the feel of being Gertrude Stein, no harm done — probably. But stiletto heels are inappropriate on writers of any gender.

NARROWING THE OPTIONS

Now that you have chosen your wardrobe, gathered your reference books, and informed your family that you won't be available for six months, it is time to decide: What *kind* of creative writing do you want to do?

Yes, there are lots of choices. They range from the highly commercial to the purely recreational, the supplemental to the masturbatory. Here is a list of some possible genres:

- Novel
- Kids' lit
- Young adult novel
- Chick lit
- Autobiography (*not* the life history of an auto)
- Travel (rent-a-camel)
- History (no fewer than twelve hundred pages)
- Medical (requires author to have a degree in something personal)

- Personal essay
- Screenplay (appropriate to one thousand videos)
- Stage play
- Poetry (commercially limited to greeting cards, but cost-effective in regard to not needing a haircut)
- Journalism (sometimes called "the Fourth Estate," because part of you has died)
- Humour (a very chancy genre unless your name is Woody Allen or Dave Barry)
- Income tax return

NOVEL

Not just the short story on steroids, the novel is a relatively recently evolved species of creative writing, still treated with contempt by some older literary critics. Even the noun was unknown until the sixteenth century when the Italian *novella* was introduced to Western Europe, along with the pepperoni pizza.

For centuries the novel form was monopolized by male writers such as Daniel Defoe and Samuel Richardson. Women were waiting for the invention of the printing press, which boosted book sales enough to make novel writing competitive with prostitution. Mary Shelley, the author of *Frankenstein*, made a bigger killing than her monster, inspiring female novelists everywhere to create heroes who needed to be struck by lightning.

Today virtually all successful novelists can be clinically identified as female. The exception being Stephen King (horror has no gender). The bestselling of these novels is called chick lit (with apologies to the chewing gum). They are stories written by women, about women, for women who have tried real men and moved on. You shouldn't attempt chick lit if you are a virgin or otherwise sexually impaired. (Another test: can you write with your legs crossed?)

If you feel that you don't meet any of these criteria, it doesn't mean you are totally lacking in sensitivity and should be writing parking tickets. Your talent may be *juvenile*, and better suited to writing books for children.

KIDS' LIT

This is a tremendously lucrative market for writers who have refused to grow up. Reason: parents are frantically buying books for their children in a desperate if futile effort to dislodge them from the Internet. Having to compete with porn channels is a real challenge to the children's author trying to create a bedtime story that doesn't involve handcuffs.

In order to write for children, it helps to *think* like a child, without having previously played professional hockey without a helmet. Some frequently asked questions about kids' lit:

Q: I'm a guy. Won't people look at me funny if I try to write children's books?

A: Of course. That's why you need to write under another name (*nom de plume*). Charles Dodgson, a respected English mathematician, could never have written *Alice's Adventures in Wonderland*. As Lewis Carroll, he did. Just make sure your literary alias hasn't already been taken (e.g., Mark Twain).

Q: Should I avoid using words of more than one syllable?

A: Not at all. Most kids over twelve can handle two syllables, sometimes more. But polysyllables may cause incontinence in sensitive children.

Q: Where can I research children's books without having to buy one?

A: Your public library. A librarian will be happy to direct you to the shelf where the children's books would be if they weren't out. Or you may browse in a children's bookstore, though some managers get shirty if you bring a camp stool.

Q: What about nursery rhymes? Any market?

A: This little piggy didn't make it. The problem with nursery rhymes is that it is difficult to write any new ones without having them, under analysis, reveal the author's sexual perversion (e.g., "Jack and Jill went up the hill" has a motivation other than to "fetch a pail of water").

YOUNG ADULT NOVEL

This is a relatively new genre of creative writing: books aimed at the special market of parents who want to give their teenager something of a legal substance.

The prototype of the young adult novel has long been the works of Horatio Alger, Jr. (1832–1899), whose boys' books inspired a whole generation of young Americans to go forth and earn big bucks. Alger's classic — *Ragged Dick* — despite the catchy title is little read by today's teenagers, being one long endorsement of hard work as a source of wealth. Alger also gave away much of his earnings to street kids, dying poor himself. Perhaps he's not a role model for those students drawn to YA novel writing in lieu of gainful employment.

YA novels are usually published in soft cover, a hint that your work may not have the longevity of the Dead Sea Scrolls. And the royalties are apt to be less than what the publisher paid the illustrator. But the glory is all yours, Horatio.

CHICK LIT

This genre is deplored as demeaning to novels in general. These novels are typically written by female authors, read mostly by women, and critically reviewed by men who like to live dangerously.

Unlike male-written novels, which are sometimes about something other than sex, chick lit concentrates almost entirely on *relationships*. It is impossible to imagine a Roberta Crusoe. Even if the castaway has email.

The genre was formerly described as "the bodice ripper." Perhaps because today no one is quite sure what a bodice is, there seems to be less ripping going on than in the days when women wore discernible vests. Also, the provocation for shredding a woman's underwear ("No!") has waned as a response to male ardour. Today it is more likely to be the guy who gets his shirt totalled by impassioned fingers. *Autre temps, autre skivvies.*

To author chick lit, a woman really needs to have a personal background of bad experience with her mother. If she hasn't had a mother, she is working at a distinct disadvantage. She will also need to have had an aunt, grandmother, or older sister to provide the oppressive regime when she is creating a female protagonist that will resonate with the reader who has relatives.

Here care must be taken, lest a wicked stepmother emerge from the closet to sue the author for libel. In fact, the author of chick lit may need to write off all her kin, in terms of amicable relations. It is the price one pays for writing fiction that isn't kept entirely outdoors.

Can a male author write chick lit? What if he is a bit effeminate? Secretly paints his toenails? Hates ice hockey? Well, probably not. Virginia Woolf said that there is a spot at the back of every woman's head the size of a shilling that no man ever sees. What she meant was that some areas of feminine sensibility are so esoteric that a guy can't access them without straining his maleness.

Although it is more natural for a female author to produce chick lit, the question is: Is it proper to exploit relatives for the purpose of producing a book? The answer: absolutely. One can't work a gold mine without disturbing the terrain, creating a certain amount of detritus. If your mother didn't want to have a daughter who uses her as the basis of a story character with the disposition of a tarantula, she should have taken proper measures to prevent conception.

However, it *is* prudent to change all names to protect the guilty.

AUTOBIOGRAPHY

This is the story of your life (sorry, *Dear Me* has been taken as a title) and should include the parts you would prefer not to be made public. These will make you look human, a quality attractive to your readers.

Should you change the names of persons in your life with whom you have had intimate or illicit relations? Never! Being sued for libel is the hallmark of a successful autobiography. As long as you don't have any assets that can be seized by the court, the litigant will soon abandon seeking redress for your having publicly identified him (or her) as a sexual deviant with a lively interest in whips, chains, and power tools.

Autobiographies are often *ghostwritten*, especially for celebrities who, for one reason or another, haven't learned how to compose whole sentences. You can earn good money as a ghostwriter, and of course the bedsheet is a lot cheaper than having to buy clothes.

TRAVEL

People like to read about voyages of discovery to exotic lands beyond East Toronto. Unfortunately, exotic lands are dwindling in number as more natives get cable. It is hard to spin an exciting narrative out of an encounter with a fearsome-looking African who is chatting on a cellphone.

Thus it is prudent to research how much has already been published about your destination. Mount Everest, for example, has been climbed to death. You don't want to learn this after you have already booked the Sherpa guides (who, of course, now also have an agent).

Second, the travel writer needs to have a camera, especially if the project is an article for *National Geographic*. The camera should be as small as possible. Reason: in some sheltered parts of the world the natives see the camera as a devilish device for extracting their souls. Being strung up with your own camera strap is an ugly way to go, even if the photos have good detail.

As for financial reward, the market for your travel writing may be limited to your community newspaper, but your trip to Fiji will be tax-deductible.

HISTORY

To succeed in this genre of writing you need to have a good working relationship with the past. This may be why history is more popular with readers than with writers. Yes, *history takes work*. It involves *substance. Legal* substance. History requires research, a task that can propel a person into the library stacks where he ages quickly. In severe cases he is never seen again.

Writing history also means getting intimate with *footnotes*, each having to be numbered by hand because your computer balks at words with a dinky digit riding on their tails.[1]

1. Like that.

Footnotes have a special attraction for non-fiction authors with a fondness for the appendix (footnote fetish), as well as for Latin abbreviations (*ibid., op. cit., etc.*) that only irritate the reader who has been looking forward to turning the page. The writer should use footnotes only as required to acknowledge the sources of his *facts*, should his history happen to include any.

By far the most popular type of history is that of a war, preferably a world war. The First and Second World Wars have been pretty well done to death, unfortunately, but new wars are breaking out all the time — some of them with the potential of becoming World War III and the end of civilization as we know it. Which could, of course, affect sales of your history book.

MEDICAL

You really do need to have your M.D. to author a bestselling book for people eager to ignore their own doctor's advice. Luckily, there are several universities that will grant the degree after completion of a correspondence course in heart surgery.

One of the most popular medical subjects today is sado-masochism, as a fun way of abusing the body without having to be drafted into the National Hockey League. Until recently, there was some stigma to being identified as a latter-day Marquis de Sade, but today there are numerous clubs for people who enjoy screaming in a social atmosphere. Researching this material may require some expenditure for gear popularized by the Spanish Inquisition, but should be tax-deductible if accompanied by degrading photos.

PERSONAL ESSAY

Montaigne is credited with having created this introverted literary form as a clever way of avoiding hard work. He could afford to, having been born rich. So, unless you expect to inherit a château in a lush part of France, depending on the sale of a book of essays may be an early symptom of dementia.

Like the diary form associated with Samuel Pepys, it's a case of "Don't give up your day job."

However, you do have the role model of America's most cherished essayist, Henry David Thoreau. Living in a simple cabin on Walden Pond, Thoreau didn't entertain much other than the ducks. His livelihood depended mostly on doing yardwork for Ralph Waldo Emerson, another essayist. Such was the Golden Era of Essayists in

America before they all joined the staff of *Time* magazine and forgot about writing earthy homilies like: "Some circumstantial evidence is very strong, as when you find a trout in the milk."

Thoreau wrote most of his best stuff in his *journal*. This assured him *posthumous* fame, which isn't as rewarding as being somebody while you are still alive.

SCREENPLAY

Here dwelleth the Big Bucks. Film producers spare no expense to obtain a screenplay for the film director to ignore once shooting starts. The screenwriter must shed all sensitivity and feel comfortable selling his soul to the highest bidder. He is, after all, relieved of responsibility for the final product, left to merely wince as the credits roll by on a violated screen.

This raises the question: Is it possible to maintain complete artistic integrity and still afford to buy food?

Instead of pondering this question, the smart screenwriter must find satisfaction in being part of the process of elimination — he must have the integrity of a turd.

It is now possible to take a university course in screenwriting and study models drawn from the kind of movies that are no longer being made. *Any* college course that doesn't have calculus as a prerequisite is bound to boost a writer's self-esteem if he avoids writing the final exam.

Also, there is a good chance you will form a relationship with a classmate, an affair that ends unhappily when the classmate turns out to be bisexual, thus providing you with dramatic scenes that would have been inconceivable had you taken a correspondence course.

STAGE PLAY

This form of creative writing worked quite well for Shakespeare, and there is no reason why you shouldn't follow in his footsteps — if you have a really long stride.

The main drawback to writing stage plays is that they nearly always involve *spoken words*. A screenplay can be successful with a minimum of verbal exchange — as proven by the Olympian stature of Governor Arnold Schwarzenegger. But it is difficult to have characters onstage without somebody's saying something. Otherwise what you have is *pantomime*, a genre pretty well restricted to an audience that still wets its pants. The main benefit from writing for the stage is not financial but social, as the playwright gets to meet a lot of people — director, actors, stagehands — whom he might otherwise never have hated.

(Note: since the Age of Aquarius has pretty well dried up, presenting nudity onstage is no longer a novelty and rarely substitutes for dialogue.)

Occasionally, a stage play first mounted in the boonies (e.g., Canada) will graduate to Broadway, off-Broadway, farther-off-Broadway, the Great White Wail, Bad Times Squared, or some other doomed site. For New York critics the only good plays Canadians make are on the ice of a hockey arena.

POETRY

Early in life nearly everyone discovers that some words rhyme with other words. This incites the young person to write what he believes to be poetry but is, in fact, the mental equivalent of a wet dream.

For most writers this is just a phase, the acne of literary puberty. They recover from it without permanent damage to their ability to express themselves on paper. In fact, Sir Arthur Quiller-Couch, the dean of budding scribes, recommends verse writing as a good exercise for the mind that has a tendency to wander into blank prose.

We might also recall that in the heyday of Greek literature, the

Olympic Games included a public reading of original verse, something hard to imagine as an element of the Grey Cup or the Super Bowl.

The main advantage that today's poet has over the ancient Greek is that modern poems may be — indeed, *should* be — comprehensible to no one but the author. Freed from the strictures of rhyme scheme and grammar, the poem reflects the breakdown of Western civilization. It draws praise from critics who recognize that it transmits the inexpressible, being as impenetrable as a mother superior.

However, the novice should understand that very few poets today can make a living from this activity alone. Even Ovid — a top-ranked poet in his time — was moonlighting from his job as a lawyer. Which of these activities led to his being exiled to the city on the Black Sea where he died, we don't know. But the message for today's aspiring poet is clear: unless you are independently wealthy or happy to be housed in an abandoned piano crate, with the Muse, you lose.

That said, if you do take a turn for the verse, and just can't resist rhyming couplets instead of leaving them alone, you may derive a lot of perfectly legal pleasure from penning an ode. (An ode is a poem meant to be sung, which may be going too far in a shaky relationship.)

JOURNALISM

This is sometimes called "the Fourth Estate," the other Three Estates being Lords Spiritual (the heads of churches), Lords Temporal (the peerage), and the Commons (the rabble). Also called "ink-stained wretches," today's journalist rarely comes into contact with ink. Instead he has an intimate relationship with a computer, which is likely to become insanely jealous if the journalist goes to the toilet.

The main virtue of journalism is that it combines creative writing with *a steady job*. An actual livelihood. Which in turn makes the writer able to afford a spouse, children, a motorized vehicle, and possibly a permanent residence with indoor plumbing.

Journalists — whether in print or electronic media — comprise the major class of employed writers today. There are actual schools of journalism and university courses to train the average writer to transmit news or opinion without attracting undue attention to himself. These courses may be combined with athletics, such as rugby, to train the reporter to take notes in a media scrum or while hanging on to the door of a politician's limo.

The basic college course for journalism is that of writing emissions for the campus student newspaper. The student — naturally shy and socially inept — gains confidence in his ability to write for an audience other than his immediate family, as well as to drink beer with other introverts.

Today the college newspaper's editorial room isn't as anarchic as in earlier times when it served as a mating ground for the creatively queer. Some observers fear that it has become merely a mirror, in miniature, of the daily newspaper, decorum snuffing out the divine afflatus.

However, writing for the student paper does familiarize a person with the hierarchy of the trade:

- cub reporter
- editorial writer
- star columnist
- publisher
- paper carrier (without whom revelation remains with St. John the Divine)

While less prestigious than being an award-winning novelist or an esteemed historian, being a journalist does get the writer out of the ivory tower and into the pub. With enough wampum to pay for a round. And seeing your name as a byline *is* visible proof of your existence in case you have doubts based on buying lottery tickets.

HUMOUR

Canadian humour is more personal than American humor because it includes *u*. (A little orthographic joke, there. We'll hurry on.)

The best-known Canadian humorist to achieve wealth, as well as fame, was Stephen Leacock. Leacock profited so handsomely from work like his *Sunshine Sketches of a Little Town* that he was able to give up his day job as a McGill University professor to concentrate entirely on making Canadians laugh — a feat previously thought to be impossible.

Today most publishers are leery of humorists because humour may be used to suggest that a sacred cow is yielding bullshit. Thus the market for humour in print has shrunk with the gelding of *Punch* and the bloated state of *The New Yorker* without Robert Benchley, James Thurber, and S.J. Perelman. Only Dave Barry survives, by the sheer weight of giggles, and he may yet be targeted by the CIA.

A pity this; in earlier times the only member of a powerful king's court who could imply folly was his clown. Not sure you will look good in motley? Take heart from Woody Allen, the humorist who added a new dimension to appearing dishevelled. Woody is the role model for the neurotic image that people find hilarious.

Does this mean that if you suspect you lack the vital neuroses, you should forget about writing humour? Probably. But there is always the chance that life will deal you a blow you can see the funny side of. If necessary, go into politics.

INCOME TAX RETURN

This form of fiction may be safely ignored by most writers. Tax-wise, their earnings put them in a bracket that is off the wall and in the basement.

However, in the blissful event that your novel hits the bestseller list or your screenplay is honoured at an Academy Awards ceremony,

it is prudent to keep a written record of all deductible expenses. Does this mean having children? Only if you are terminally fertile. Dependents are the most costly type of tax deduction. Especially if your children are over forty and living at home.

Tax-wise, it is better to have a liver transplant than to have children (liquor is deductible if used to research a project).

While using your creative imagination to prepare your tax return, it is wise to remember that the Receiver General can be a severe critic.

His unfavourable review of your work could include a cash penalty and possibly a jail sentence. Yes, your new computer may be deductible if used for something other than browsing the Internet for porn. But the trip to Tahiti to research a book on Paul Gauguin's use of native girls may not survive scrutiny (unless artfully woven into a travel narrative).

So, with math skills unequipped to deal with numbers over ten, it may be prudent for the writer, in the unusual circumstance of his having earned money, to have his tax return prepared by a tax accountant. One who is willing to do the job in return for having his car washed.

MODUS OPERANDI

Now that you have chosen the kind of creative writing you wish to do, and written it down as a reminder in case you start to drift off into doodling or worse, what *gear* do you need besides the stout eraser?

A **computer**. As mandated earlier in this lecture, this has to be the most important relationship in a writer's life. Yet, and as incredible as it may seem to us today, much of our past literature was created without the aid of a computer. Writers such as Shakespeare, Samuel Johnson, and even Charles Dickens wrote what they did with no laptop other than the one made when they sat down. What they wrote was not by the grace of Bill Gates. So how did they do it and still produce very acceptable written work?

Examination of old *manuscripts* — from the Latin words for "hand" and "written" — reveals that all of this peerless material was written with **pen and ink**. Yes, they didn't even have a ballpoint to chew. Writers had to dip their "pen" — often little more than a turkey feather renamed "quill" — into a bottle of murky liquid. Dozens of times a page. The quill had no delete button. This meant that the writer had to *think* before he wrote. Otherwise the page looked really messy, which is the main reason why most of the early writers were monks depending on divine guidance.

Now, some antiquarians argue that handwriting gave the writer the *feel* of the words he was using, the rhythm of a sentence, the concerto of the paragraph.

Twaddle! Writers were composing on the typewriter — a clackety device with no warning of misspellings — for years without loss of lyricism or other ill effect except the increase in alcoholism.

True, there *is* some clinical evidence that it is prudent to write a first draft in **pencil**, then transfer the text to the computer. Reason: the computer has been known to lose an entire novel. A critique, perhaps, but one that the writer didn't ask for.

WORK HAZARDS

Most writers prefer to go straight to work on their computer, right after checking their email. (Reading email and feasting on spam —the gratuitous messaging from persons or humanoids to whom we haven't been formally introduced — can occupy a writer fully until it is time for a coffee break).

The distraction of email, along with surfing the Internet, enables the writer to delay, or possibly avoid entirely, the serious work of composition. It is possible to email the same information to hundreds of people — family, friends, even total strangers — which is a level of market saturation the writer may never match with his *other* written work. His reward is, of course, not financial but the gratitude of the email recipients, who read it as an excuse for delaying or avoiding their own work.

It is conservatively estimated that email, worldwide, eliminates more millions of hours of useful toil than any recreation since the golf course.

It is normal to fake indignation at having our time wasted by persons to whom we aren't related by blood or natural bonding. A writer may actually go straight from his email to creating a graphic scene of murder, or sadistic sex, with renewed zest.

Another reliable source of distraction is your *printer*. This device has come a long way since William Caxton, in fifteenth-century England, created a new source of typographical errors: printing. Today's home printer has vastly increased the number of ways in which something can go wrong. It also vomits paper at a rate that is accelerating the deforestation of the planet. Most of these pages are blank, for reasons known only to the printer, and of course the printer repairman, who has replaced our other relationships.

As for your copier/fax machine, forget about sex — this is the only reproduction you can afford.

WHERE TO WRITE

Now that you have defined what kind of writing you would like to do and bought the hardware necessary to this mission, *where* is the best place to perform the actual act of composition? Not everyone can afford the luxury of a private study guarded by a sign on the door: NO ADMISSION! GENIUS AT WORK!

If the writer is fortunate enough to have an actual desk in his home, with a bottom drawer to accommodate all amassed rejections, he has no excuse for using it only as a footrest. A chair that swivels in response to any interruption of work is optional.

Only very successful writers who can afford the vasectomy or hysterectomy to eliminate the possibility of intrusion by children can count on prolonged seclusion for intercourse with the Muse.

Locking yourself in the bathroom with your laptop is feasible only if other family members will respect your privacy and use a commode.

The outhouse is a prime location on which to put pencil to paper while waiting for the bowels to respond to the call of nature. It is impossible to estimate how many immortal lines have been generated in this austere accommodation. For all we know Hamlet's gloomy reflection, "To be or not to be," was inspired by Shakespeare's sojourn in the bog.

If all else fails, the public library is another place where you can find a place to sit, though you may have to borrow a book from time to time to ward off a shirty librarian.

THE ART OF ACTUAL WRITING

Okay, you have now decided what kind of creative writing you want to get it on with, you have collected the technical equipment needed to convey this to a waiting world, and you've secured a place to write. You are ready to commence the actual process of producing *organized words*.

Despite all the technological advances in creative writing since the ancient Egyptians chipped out obituary notices in royal tombs, it is still defined as *art*. It is not a science. The writer's mind is constantly fighting off fact in favour of fancy. He is wide open to inspiration, that magical force that causes him to leap out of bed — regardless of company — to capture the divine afflatus ere it fly into oblivion. In writing.

A close examination of our literature reveals that most writing consists of *words*. The words used are the product of *selection* (otherwise, Noah Webster would be the greatest author of all time).

The writer selects words from his *vocabulary*. In fact, it is impossible to exaggerate the importance of vocabulary in creative writing. The writer's vocabulary is like a nursing mother's breast: the larger it is, the more you get out of it.

If a person's vocabulary consists almost entirely of words, where does he *obtain* these words? Some of our words may be found in a standard dictionary, while others derive from other motorists. But most of our words are extracted from books, magazines, and newspapers. Yes, reading fertilizes writing. Television, being relatively inarticulate, does little for vocabulary and even less for spelling. Radio, worse, as one can't read lips. As for the Internet, vocabulary is in a dot coma. All menu and little nutrition.

Reading! It is a fact that reading almost always involves words, outside of China. Some of these words have more than one syllable. Read these words often enough and eventually their meaning will sink in, becoming a usable part of the vocabulary you need to keep handy for writing.

Don't fret about spelling. Correcting spelling is your editor's job and is the reason she makes more money than you do. Likewise punctuation. (Fussing over punctuation is donkey work and will be further ignored in the section on style. However, if you have a serious addiction to the semicolon, you may need personal counselling.)

Concern yourself with the important task of choosing, what the French call *le mot juste*, or the *exact* word, with a pickiness usually associated with selecting the right dinner wine. If you drink plonk regardless of what you are scoffing up for supper, you may carry this laxity into your writing. If we had to fight a cork to access our vocabulary, we all might be more attentive, appraising every word for its robust or subtle colour ... bouquet ... unique taste. It may help to think of yourself as a literary sommelier. Apron optional.

It is equally important to use *active* verbs rather than passive, overweight, or otherwise indolent layabout verbs. Because the verb is essential to the description of action, it is hard to write a novel, for instance, without using a verb at some point in the story. If verbs make you nervous, it may be prudent to confine your writing to government reports, greeting cards, and dinner menus.

As for nouns, their worth shouldn't be judged on the basis of how many syllables they contain. Just because your vocabulary happens to include a word of more than two syllables isn't reason enough to work that word into every sentence.

It is better to build a sentence with *concrete* nouns rather than those of the abstract variety, which should be reserved for writing philosophy, economics, or family letters. (A concrete word evokes something we can see, smell, hear, touch, or apprehend while sober.)

Nouns may also be divided — after some initial confusion — into *proper* nouns or *improper* nouns. Proper nouns are found mostly in non-fiction, improper nouns in public washrooms, along with improper verbs and improper adjectives (aka ejaculations).

A noun may also be a *gerund*, which is a verb masquerading as a noun. The gerund used to be a *declinable* noun, but now it says yes to everything. A sign of the general moral decline of society?

So what about those so-called *dirty words*? How do you:

1. Identify a trope as truly filthy?
2. Avoid the overuse of obscenities for their shock value?
3. Judge their suitability in a children's book?

These shady elements of vocabulary are often called "four-letter words" because a careful audit does confirm that most, if not all, contain four letters.

Without doubt the most problematic, especially in kids' books, is "the eff-word." Since the eff-word is one of the most frequently used locutions — especially in heavy traffic — and demonstrates amazing versatility ("eff off," "eff all," "eff up," and of course the last word in intimacy, "eff you"), it requires a conscious effort to spare your computer this phrase it has heard all too often.

However, the writer shouldn't shrink from calling a spade a *spade* unless, of course, it is a *shovel*, which has a somewhat different shape.

STYLE

Now that you have a decent supply of words, sorted and laundered for a public appearance, how do you assemble them to provide maximum effect?

First, they gotta have *rhythm.*

Just because today's poets have rejected rhythm as a vestige of giving the reader pleasure, there's no reason for other writers not to make it an element of their style. In moderation. But not the rhythm of the lullaby. Excessive rhythm should be confined to church service homilies and company boardroom reports.

Remember: the message travels from the eye to the brain via the ear, possibly with a pit stop at the genitals.

Today the sonorous rhythms of the Victorian novelist — and even Charles Dickens could be pure Ovaltine — have given way to those of faster-paced prose and staccato verse. The violin section has been turfed in favour of the percussion. Think of your pen as a jackhammer. If it helps, write wearing a hard hat.

Some literary analysts believe that rhythm is something a writer is born with in lieu of common sense. If you can dance, you can waltz through a compound sentence.

The pleasurable pacing of your prose — a phrase demonstrating that *alliteration* can be a sedative — depends very much on your cunning use of *punctuation*.

Punctuation is like the neighbourhood pub: it can be either "open" or "closed," and is often a factor in alcoholism.

Although it is best not to become a fanatic about your punctuation, there have been ugly scenes resulting from arguments about abuse of the exclamation mark (!), aka "the schoolgirl shriek," as emphasis rather than exclamation ("'Shit!' cried the Duchess"). But certain rules do apply:

1. Reserve the question mark (?) for completed interrogation. It should not be used internally. ("My friend [?] ran off with my wife"). Cute punctuation is largely responsible for the high suicide rate among editors.
2. The assertive sentence has its period (.) regardless of whether it is pregnant with meaning.
3. No one uses the semicolon (;) anymore. The difference between a pause (comma) and a full stop (on the dot) has become too subtle for today's faster-paced writing.
4. *Italics* may add emphasis and a dash of Chianti but could cause your computer to overheat.

Remember: "the style is the man himself" (Buffon, a certified eighteenth-century count). Your writing style says a lot about you as a person. It can reveal you as a Scrooge (closed punctuation), or demonstrate that you are a generous soul in whose mouth butter would refuse to melt (the vowels of compassion).

Don't count on your computer to sweeten your style. That bitch is just waiting to demonstrate that, with you, the style is the monster.

FIGURES OF SPEECH

Despite the name, we don't need to be speaking in order to use figures of speech. They can work equally well in writing. *In moderation.* Excessive use of simile or metaphor can slow a novel down to a snail's pace. (See? that one snuck in right there.) This can be absolutely fatal to a screenplay, let alone a financial report.

The two most abused figures of speech are the *simile* and the *metaphor.* "Quick as a flash" is an example of a simile that has gone into menopause. (A metaphor there, possibly offensive, for demonstration purpose only.)

The difference between a simile and a metaphor is that a simile says that something is *like* something else, whereas a metaphor says that something *is* something … else. (That definition may be clear as mud — right? [Another simile ready for burial.]) And here we have a demonstration — fully deserving of a footnote, if this work had feet — of how brackets and parentheses may be used to titillate the reader who relishes confinement.

Both similes and metaphors have been used by writers for centuries in order to create a *picturesque* style. This method of creating pictures has gone into decline with the arrival of *television,* which of course conveys pictures without having to hold a book while strumming one's lip.

Today's writer leaves more to the reader's *imagination,* which is normally more lurid than anything the writer could picture without having his work banned by school libraries.

Instead of graphic description the writer may turn to *hyperbole.* Hyperbole is very effective for *humour.* Woody Allen is a master of comedic hyperbole: "… her figure described a set of parabolas that could cause cardiac arrest in a yak."

Hyperbole is used almost exclusively for fun, but may cause an allergic reaction in a reader who is unfamiliar with exaggeration.

A safer tool for humorous effect is *understatement*. This is an English, rather than American, device and should be served with a cup of tea with lemon.

GRAMMAR

This is not, as most of us know, Grandpa's wife.

But what of the questions: Does correct grammar interfere with creativity? Or, may grammar itself be creative, introducing novel relationships between subject and verb?

Certainly, the rules of grammar are now more flexible than in the days when Fowler was ordering stiffer sentences than a criminal court judge with a toothache. In his *Modern English Usage*, Fowler is especially hard on the *dangling participle*. He verifies that this pendulous construction can induce more gratuitous hilarity in a reader than perhaps any other blooper: "The girl grabbed the steering wheel from him and, causing a loss of control, he was killed in the crash."

This kind of unattached construction results from trying to cram more into a sentence than it can reasonably accommodate. This is another reason why successful writers today mostly adopt a simple style that avoids the participle as a grammatical land mine, primed to blow up an otherwise dignified paragraph.

How much should a creative writer depend on an editor to correct his grammar? Answer: as little as possible. Most editors are writers in need of gainful employment. They don't edit just for the joy of salvation; they are in a correction facility. They can't wait to get out the minute another editor finds their work publishable. (See section on **Editors**.)

INVENTION

No, we are not talking here about the latest technical gizmo to accelerate your Internet consumption. You are probably already spending too much of your morning deleting yesterday's stroke of genius, or forming attachments less than lifelong.

Inventive writing is that which *says something new*. An impossible goal, you may protest, given the sheer volume of verbiage being discharged into the atmosphere. How, you ask, do I know for sure that what I am writing hasn't already been done, possibly better, by someone with a creative lawyer?

"Great minds think alike" won't satisfy a judge.

The best way to avoid subconscious plagiarism is, of course, to read nothing. But don't depend on the belief that pinching material is hard to prove if you have taken the precaution of changing the punctuation.

All's fair in love and war, but in writing you need to be careful. And to resort to that more estimable source of creativity: *imagination*. Even if the author has led a remarkably adventurous life, crowded with incidents and relationships that provide a bushel of grist for the mill, this will need to be leavened with imagination for it to make real dough. (Note the example of an extended metaphor that may strain the reader's patience.)

IMAGINATION

Imagination is the mind's eye. For too many writers it's an optical illusion. So how does the writer come by a lively imagination? Is it something he is born with? Or is it the product of a sheltered childhood? Does it grow, like the pearl in the oyster, as a result of a confined and irritating social environment? Or is it just a way for the mind to compensate for what the body is missing? Nature's reward, for example, for remaining a virgin while normal people were having fun?

Are you a naturally shy person? Yes? Congratulations! You have met the first requirement of writerly imagination. You have been keeping all your sex fantasies in your head rather than in motels. At first blush this may not seem as exciting as meeting a really charming nymphomaniac in a bar, or a nice naval officer on the beach. But on the plus side you have reduced your chances of contracting a quite tedious venereal disease.

Imagination is less of a factor if we are writing non-fiction (which may include autobiography). Most other literary genres do depend on the author's imagination, something harder to measure when sober.

Imagination is especially vital if the writer has been leading a cloistered life. Very few fictional bestsellers are written by nuns or monks.

"Living it up, so that you can write it down" is a formula that requires examination before leaping — in the larger context of avoiding arrest on charges of illicit sex with a minor while operating a vehicle under the influence of an illegal substance.

With due respect to poet Dylan Thomas, literary invention isn't a genie in a bottle. Or a brothel. The trick is to live a full life without spilling any. Female authors seem to be better at this than the guys, who tend to prefer not to draw on their sexual experience unless writing comedy.

AIDS TO INSPIRATION

One genre that is especially dependent on personal experience is the *travel book*. It is very difficult to write an effective travel book without, at some point, getting out of the house. Casanova's memoirs take him all over Europe, affording him international access to women and phenomena he would never have experienced had he stayed in the Italian jail.

(Note: *memoirs* are a special category of writing, less popular today than in the days when people wanted to record what they were doing with their lives. Also, the laws of libel constrain public recounting of romantic adventures. In fact, you can't even narrate an amusing episode from a Tibetan guest house without expecting a formal letter from a Lhasa law firm.)

Now, if you don't have much imagination (especially on Monday mornings), you may be tempted to enhance the modicum by using a controlled substance. Luckily, most substances (alcohol, pot, Italian coffee) are out of control these days in the Western world. But certain hard drugs serve as an accelerant of imagination only at considerable risk to other parts of the brain that may be needed for essential services, such as tying your shoelaces or operating a vehicle.

Far too many writers buy their imagination at the liquor store.

"Solitude is as needful to the imagination as society is wholesome for the character," wrote James Russell Lowell. Solitude isn't hard to come by, especially if the writer lacks access to a bath. But, like other stimulants, solitude can be overdone. Being alone all the time, and depending on cable television for the raw material of your sex scenes or for really anything but a catalogue of cooking recipes, can severely limit creativity.

RAW MATERIALS

Essential to every creative writer is some experience of life. This usually means getting out of the house for longer than to pick up the newspaper from the porch. Very little happens on the porch, in most neighbourhoods, with which to flesh out a novel.

"Living it up in order to write it down," as I mentioned, is a formula that should involve buying accident insurance. Which may not be tax-deductible. But grist to the mill is not a closet harvest.

True, some fiction writers — not many, but a noteworthy few — have achieved literary success without looking for material outside their study. Virginia Woolf, for instance, by all accounts didn't get out much socially, but lived inside her own head, probably a contributing factor in her ending up afloat in the river, sadly deceased.

On the other hand, it is easy to excuse an extravagant social life as a source of raw material. During the 1930s, swarms of American novelists descended on Paris, a site believed to be the motherlode of uninhibited sexual adventure. Later, after Hitler had cooled off Paris as *the* horny pilgrimage destination, some North American writers made the hegira to Mexico, where the siesta is institutionalized as a major element of the workday. This mecca has since waned in popularity, however, as the peso woke up and started acting like real money.

More recently, the Far North (anywhere *not* south of Toronto) has attracted travel writers who have an independent source of thermal underwear. Inuit no longer bother hunting seals, finding it easier to skin the writers herding poleward in search of frostbite.

For the neophyte novelist, the *terra incognita* lies in troubled relationships with other mammals. Especially people. But how can you be sure the other person isn't just using *you* as the basis for a character given to weird sexual behaviour? Some ominous signs:

- Your subject asks to borrow your pen while you are engaged in intercourse.
- She, or he, insists that your romantic camping trip won't be complete without a tape recorder.
- You have reason to suspect that your subject calls you "darling" because she is unable to remember your name.

All things considered, there is good reason for concentrating on some other species as novel material, even at the risk of being suspected of bestiality. Very few dogs can afford to hire a lawyer.

WHAT'S *NOT* APPROPRIATE

Whatever it is that you are writing — novel, newspaper editorial, in fact, anything but a shopping list — it is essential to maintain the same tone throughout. Many a person voicing the eulogy at the funeral of a loved one has yielded to the impulse to tell a funny story. Very rarely does this aberration succeed, the yarn joining the deceased.

Reason: the interjection was *inappropriate*. Like wearing sneakers with a tuxedo, the attention it draws is negative. This is why good writing is as much resistance to impulse as it is response to inspiration. Yes, it takes a strong will to reject the pun that begs for admittance to your article on male impotence. But writing is not for those who, like Oscar Wilde, can resist anything but temptation.

Another shallow in the stream of consciousness is *imitation*. Which, sayeth the old saw, is the sincerest form of flattery. But if what we write imitates the work of someone else, particularly a person who isn't deceased and has access to a lawyer, the flattery may get lost in litigation.

Plagiarism. This is an offence to be avoided at all (including legal) cost. Yet it is easy, nay, natural, to borrow entire sentences, if not paragraphs, from another's work and forget to grace them with quotation marks. Not all of us have a photographic memory, Your Honour. We remember some things better than others. And sometimes the subconscious mind rides roughshod over assiduity so that before we know it we have written deathless prose that has already joined the immortal.

JARGON

Word-wise, not every sentence serves the writer, but too often the writer should be serving a sentence. For committing *jargon*.

Jargon — words used to impress rather than inform — corrupts non-fiction more than stories. If you are a doctor writing a book about your adventures in people's internal organs, you have to avoid *medical* jargon — one of the most potent narcotics a reader can take.

The writer is particularly susceptible to this vice if he judges his output by the number of words he has written in the day. This is called the quota syndrome. If one day he fails to write his quota — because of some nuisance like a sudden death in the immediate family, or his computer going into menopause — the writer suffers guilt. And will try to compensate the next day by doubling that day's quota, even though this severely depletes his supply of adjectives.

Using a computer compounds the risk of jargon by documenting how many words, total, the author has written in the workday. It is right there, accusingly, at the bottom of your screen: "19." Which is another argument for writing everything first in longhand: no blabbermouth word count.

Another consort of jargon cited by Quiller-Couch: the case of "in the case of." Nothing should be in the case except your bottles of lager. This is why legal briefs — the underwear of justice — are 90 percent jargon, 10 percent substance. Without jargon our system of jurisprudence would be accelerated to a pace inimical to the income of lawyers and magistrates.

However, if the writer wants to produce material for the average reader not wearing a wig, she or he will check every word to ensure that it is pulling its full weight of meaning.

To this end the writer may be tempted to *coin* words (neologism) as a surrogate for coining money. Words are minted mostly in the popular media such as newspapers or TV, or by drug companies. A bit presumptuous, therefore, for the amateur.

As a general rule, one should avoid using a word, or phrase, that draws too much attention to itself. *Cuteness.* It is sadly easy for the writer — like the party show-off who dons a lampshade — to win attention while losing respect.

Finally, words are cheap, yet are one commodity that can cost the writer dearly if not chosen with the economy of a Dutch housewife.

EMPHASIS

Not to be confused with the disease contracted from smoking tobacco or other field produce, emphasis is very important! Even if it requires the exclamation mark, aka "the schoolgirl shriek," every writer wants his work to have impact. The all-too-common devices (besides "!") to achieve this emphasis are:

1. putting certain words in *italics*
2. putting other words in CAPITALS
3. <u>underlining whole passages</u>

These contortions may be appropriate in certain literary milieus, such as the warning labels on drugs, but they rate as overkill in prose or verse aimed at adults with an IQ superior to that of a gerbil.

Other writers seek emphasis by keeping their sentences very short. Like this. Staccato. Sometimes called "Chicago style." The reader has no chance to get bored with those rapid-fire periods peppering his attention span. This terseness does have the virtue of helping to keep the reader from dozing off — one of the reasons for the drying up of the stream-of-consciousness novel.

However, there are less jerky ways of achieving emphasis. One of these, cited by Quiller-Couch, is the judicious placement of words in a sentence. Sometimes this is a matter of saving the most important word (like dessert) to the end. "The wages of sin is Death" — despite the singularity of the verb — makes mortality more final than "Death is the wages of sin."

Can this verbal skill be taught? Is it possible that, just as some folk (mostly black) seem to be born with a better sense of rhythm than people who inhabit northern parts of the Earth, timely words come more easily to writers for whom climax comes naturally, whether in bed or at the desk?

This is a matter that warrants further study, in this case by someone else. The main point: avoid prematurely ejaculating the important word. Your partner (the reader) will be better satisfied, unless of course you have contrived a very long sentence, such as this, from which it is difficult to emerge before your reader has dozed off.

The Good Book puts it succinctly: "How forcible are right words!"

THE EFF-WORD

Some writers — usually of the older generation — wonder whether they should use the eff-word in their novels or short stories. Even if they are writing dialogue as part of the scene of an auto collision or marital dispute, they still may hesitate.

Bite the bullet, ma'am.

To be true to real life, dialogue will include the eff-word in just about every sentence. It is very difficult for a character to display emotional disturbance — even that caused by a minor crisis such as a flat tire — without uttering the eff-word.

Yet it can be done. The downside: you may be restricted to writing drama for daytime television. Or a newspaper opinion column. But there is a market for work devoid of eff-less monosyllables, if these are selected with care. (*Fudge* as a surrogate is too cute to be borne.)

However, some writers pepper their work with the eff-word as a token of artistic integrity — and blame rejection on the craven media. But the hard, not to say tumescent, fact is: the eff-word has lost its shock value even for the reader who has lived a remarkably sheltered life.

Also, it would be a shame to discard a virile verb that displays such conjunctive versatility, coupling with a variety of prepositions

— "eff off," "eff up," etc. — as well as being singularly onomatopoeic.

The eff-word may, in fact, be the most versatile, as well as the most popular, verb in the English language. It just needs to be used where and when appropriate and should never serve as the mainstay of the writer's vocabulary.

This lets the writer blunder, in all good conscience, into *pornography*. The vogue of print porn has suffered greatly from the surrender of civilization to the Internet. *Smut dot com* has pretty well deleted the market for raunchy novels. Not only is a picture worth a thousand words, but we live in a time when, verbally, anything goes, as long as it doesn't affect the drinking water.

(Note: the word *pornography* derives from the Greek words *porne* [prostitute] and *grapho* [write], so that *pornography* literally means the writing of harlots. Apparently, the floozies of ancient Greece found time to write, but as yet nothing too noteworthy has emerged from Las Vegas.)

(Another note: Just as a woman can't be somewhat pregnant, a book can't be a bit pornographic. In for a shilling, in for a pound. That was the secret of the success of the Marquis de Sade, who wrote the randy novels that earned him more or less permanent residency in the Bastille. Which had pretty good room service for those who, like the count, were living off the avails of prosecution.)

READING AS A RESOURCE

Reading is *the* best way for the would-be writer to familiarize herself with words put on paper, rather than heard on television or seen in graffiti. Quiller-Couch recommends reading the classics — Homer,

Virgil, et al. in the original Greek or Latin, but this may be a tad much for the novice writer whose reading background has been limited to the menu at McDonald's.

Our mentor stresses the value of reading in absorbing the role of *vowel sounds*. If the consonants are the percussion section of our verbal orchestra, the vowels are the violins. This doesn't mean that the composer may use them with abandon (loose vowels), but that they serve as the major affective instrument in the concerto for pen and paper.

So if our Homer is more of a pop fly, what kind of reading provides the best tonic for the writer's vocabulary? The tabloid newspaper that suffices for too many readers is fashioned for mouth-breathers, folk who view words of more than one syllable as a threat to comprehension. At the other extreme are today's "critically acclaimed" novels that employ words that have a difficult relationship with their meaning, or are so arcane that even the author seems unsure of their connotation.

The classics are safer for reading. Their durability is testimony to the authors' concentrating on the story to be told, without readers having to commute to the nearest *Webster*.

The public library: that is the place to find reading that fructifies vocabulary. Walk straight past the table of latest bestsellers to the stacks that bear the classics. When you check out a work by William Makepeace Thackeray or Anton Chekhov, the librarian will look at you with new respect.

For maximum benefit this reading should be done in bed. The brain seems to benefit from having the feet somewhat elevated. The prone position, too, facilitates distribution of such blood as is flowing to the cortex, though falling asleep over your book may invoke suffocation.

What is *not* verbally salubrious is *reading on the computer*. Google is no substitute for good books. On the Internet all paths lead to naughty pictures, regardless of whether the reader set out to check a ferry or train schedule. If he or she is impoverished for human company, the Internet readily seduces the reader into an exchange of e-correspondence with another loner in Tibet — and into the delusion that this matches the quality of the letters of Bernard Shaw and Ellen Terry.

No, the computer, as an editor, has no talent beyond bugging you about your spelling. Picky, picky, picky, and not a good word to say about your punctuation.

TEAM WRITING

This is a rather special trade for the writer who is able to sublimate ego to further income. Which can be hefty enough to compensate for the loss of integrity, freedom, and a normal sex life.

Nearly all the words we hear on the Tube or read in magazines (such as *Time*) have been crafted by writers with a special talent for *le mot juste*, or catchy phrase, *honed in company*. Yes, collegial composition, without the ivy. The major market: comedy.

Several stand-up comedians (Woody Allen, Jerry Seinfeld) have become so successful they were able to sit down. And hire other writers to help them script TV series and films that rendered them millionaire status.

The downside of team comedy writing: the pressure of the weekly deadline can severely test the emotional and mental balance of the writer, resulting in temporary impotence and/or shingles. If a person is already taking medication for hypertension or piles, or is serious about giving up smoking, he or she might be well advised to consider a more contemplative medium.

For reasons not clearly understood, comedy-writing teams are usually male in composition, the members already certified as lunatic.

"Born with a gift of laughter and a sense that the world was mad" is a trait less inherent in the female gender, doubtless related to childbearing.

Because men don't have a monthly period, or don't notice it unless it happens on a weekend, the comedy writer is able to concentrate completely on the stress of working with other men to a deadline. What they are generating is likely to be the script for an episode of a TV genre called the *sitcom*, i.e., situation comedy. The writer must think in terms of episode (short-term) rather than plot (long-term, or burial).

The acknowledged masters of sketch TV were the writers of *Monty Python's Flying Circus*, most of whom appeared in the skits to their eternal profit. These masters were also *British*. So if you are not, and suspect that you are entirely rational, on the basis of your having normal relations with other people rather than horses and dogs, this species of writing may not be suitable.

Less demanding, but not much, is team writing of advertising copy, especially for television. This requires a special type of inspiration, on demand, but is the most lucrative of all the venues for prostituting talent. The career is so stressful as to be short-lived. In public you are mentally ringing a little bell and mumbling, "Unclean … unclean …"

The bottom line: if your heart is set on seeing your name as a byline, stay clear of advertising agencies. That way anonymity lies, albeit in the lap of luxury.

EDITORS – CARE AND FEEDING OF

The major drawback of having your book accepted by a publisher is that this attracts the attention of an *editor*. The word derives from the Latin *adere edit*, meaning to put out. This meaning survives in the author's feeling quite put out when the editor returns the work for correction.

It is like having your newborn — which you produced as a perfect act of creation — being brought in from the maternity ward all marked up on parts considered to need improvement. And God is mocked.

Now, the novice writer is apt to be so affronted by this gratuitous intrusion, by this nitpicking harvest, that he or she, in a double-breasted snit, is tempted to tear up the contract and send the manuscript to a different publisher.

Probably a bad idea. The second publisher may have the same editor as the first publisher, only using a different name and wearing a false moustache. And, of course, finding the same alleged blemishes on the ms. Plus a few more for spite.

The ugly fact is that publishers trust their editor's judgment more than they do the author's. Insufferable, yes. But it is a fact of literary life that must be lived with. Sticking pins in a voodoo doll won't cause your editor to shrivel up and blow away. The atrocious meddling must be tolerated. And — the plus side — may be blamed if the publication gets roasted by critics.

In murder mysteries, the butler did it. In book publication, the editor.

Chances are that your publisher will farm your manuscript out to a freelance editor, often a writer desperate for income and ready to accept any job, repugnant though it may be. If you are a freelance writer, you may be drawn into a joust of freelancers, each getting up on his high horse and levelling snide margin notes at the adversary. Monitor your blood pressure.

After the toxic dust settles, it is traditional for the author to preface the work with an expression of thanks to her or his editor. A more sincere note might be struck with: *This book was published despite gratuitous meddling by a certain person masquerading as an editor*. However, in publishing as in other relationships, honesty is not always the best policy.

Also, there is a chance that you, your writing career put on hold by a shortage of food, may find employment as a *casual* editor. The job isn't terribly well paid, considering that it has a health-hazard rating right up there with lion taming. But as long as you avoid places where authors are known to hunt for food or drink, you may earn real money. Blood money, yes, but Safeway must be served.

PUBLISHERS

Most writers hope to see their work published. Preferably in their lifetimes. There may be a few shy creatures born to blush unseen and waste their sweetness on the desert air, but they are weird.

In print. That is how any normal, ego-driven writer wants to see his or her work. Wearing a proper jacket. Sitting in a bookstore window. With the blessing of a *New York Times* book review.

So the writer needs a *publisher*. Now publishers, like bras and other projectors, come in various sizes. Some publishers are big enough to be *houses*. To have your work accepted by a publishing house is a triumph in itself, such that some writers just quit further writing rather than risk a letdown. There are no new worlds to conquer, Alex.

Most publishers, however, are more of a cottage industry, using their garages as offices because they can't afford to own cars. These smaller publishers aren't to be sneezed at unless their offices are really dusty. Many act as their own editors, so that the author's manuscript doesn't have to survive multiple judgments by people who enjoy disagreeing with one another.

In contrast, major publishers are too busy — applying for grants from government agencies and benevolent foundations — to personally read the books they publish. For that tedious and booby-trapped exercise they employ a *reader*, a person financially desperate enough to enter the minefield. The professional reader is never identified, because a rejected author is a wounded beast, ready to lunge at anyone who has questioned his use of alliteration, let alone the value of the whole text.

So what about self-publishing? If the person who acts as his own lawyer has a fool for a client, the person who acts as his own publisher has a real doofus for an author. Some people own a whole library of self-published books, of which not one copy has been sold. A touching tribute to ego, perhaps, but — desecration of forest land aside — a harmless folly. And the books provide a good place to press any flowers that you send yourself.

REJECTION!

Impossible as it may seem, as we enjoy the afterglow of birthing what we know to be a potential bestseller if not a modern classic, our work may be *rejected*. Yes, spurned by some blind-minded publisher who is obviously in the terminal phase of dementia.

We know that what we have written is damn good, probably brilliant. Family members and friends to whom we have entrusted reading a chapter or two are unequivocal in declaring — without having to read another word — that what we have done has left them speechless with wonder.

Yet some yahoo in a publisher's kennel of mad dogs has irrevocably and forever blown our respect for his judgment by *rejecting* our manuscript. That editor has doomed himself to a lifetime of ridicule, becoming known throughout the publishing world as the idiot who rejected our work.

"Thank you for submitting this material to us. Unfortunately, it does not meet our needs at this time...." The bastard doesn't say what their needs are, or even what time it is. It's a form letter, with the stamped signature carefully garbled.

Infuriating, yes. But we should try to find it in our heart to *feel sorry* for the cretin who rejected our manuscript. That reader may have been going through some personal crisis — terminal eczema, spousal infidelity, income tax audit — that temporarily deranged his judgment to the point of self-destructive lunacy.

Well, there are none so blind, etc. Let them wallow in their myopic editorial misjudgment. When you're breaking new ground as a creative writer, sometimes you strike gold, other times, garbage. The main thing: keep shovelling, podner!

PERNICKETY CRITICS

Every author, on publication, goes through three emotional stages:

1. Hoping that his/her book will receive rave reviews.
2. Wondering why his/her book has received *no* reviews.

3. Suspecting that his/her book has become the victim of a media plot to suppress writing that makes theirs look bad, styled for the lowest form of readership.

The newborn author knows that his book's getting a laudatory review from Mom, or a person who owes the author money, is not to be trusted as evaluation.

But how trustworthy is the review of your work by a complete stranger who doesn't care whether you cry easily? Here it is useful to understand that literary critics come in two varieties: professional and amateur. They are often hard to distinguish, solely by their sneer. And much of their publishing space may have been lost to TV and film reviews, making them even snarlier.

With the wane of professional literary criticism — a fairly respectable genre of nitpicking dating from Aristotle through William Hazlitt, I.A. Richards, et al. — the sometime job has fallen to a *reviewer*. This is usually a writer who is between royalty cheques and glad to get his teeth into something, having been denied a decent steak.

What the reviewer writes is called a *critique* (*cree-teek*). A certain amount of prestige is won by your work, just to have it *cree-teeked* at all. Even an unfavourable review is better than drawing no notice whatever. In fact, some people make a point of reading only books that have received a scathing review. They recognize that many book reviewers are essentially attention-seekers, people whose mission in life is to stand out from the herd, even if this means leaping off a cliff.

Another comfort: the book critic is ill paid for his work, often receiving no compensation other than the copy of the book he is reviewing. Why should the author respect the judgment of a person who is earning less than a *real* garbage collector?

Anyway, if we are unfortunate enough to have our work receive a negative book review, what should be our reaction to this pretentious drivel? First — and *memorize this counsel* — remember that a critic gains a wide reputation only by being egregiously vicious. Mr. (or Ms.) Nice Guy has no future as a book critic. The late Nathan Cohen of the *Toronto Star* gained fame as a veritable fountain of acerbic criticism. He caused more tears than an onion-peeling contest. Formidable, but he wasn't well loved by writers.

So if you have no history of pulling the wings off insects as recreation, literary criticism may not be your bent.

As for finding yourself on the receiving end of a nasty critique, you need to develop the mental epidermis of the thick-skinned. Keep a stiff upper lip. (If you have a chronically limp upper lip, you can have it stiffened surgically, but may find it harder to whistle for your dog, or a waiter.)

THE LITERARY AGENT

The agony of the rejected lover is naught compared to the anguish of the rejected author. This is reason enough to engage a literary agent to flog our work. The agent will take the brunt of the rejection by a publisher and will comfort the author with a second opinion, such as that the publisher has suffered a mental breakdown, blinding him to our unique talent.

It is, of course, possible for the author to be rejected by a literary agent. There is no shame in this, and it is certainly not grounds for jumping off a bridge unless you have additional sources of acute depression.

However, it is difficult to overestimate the value of having an agent. Especially an agent who has a good track record, among publishers, for submitting potential bestsellers. The agent is assumed to have screened out the garbage so that the publisher is, in effect, providing a second opinion and can head to the golf course earlier.

Because of the complexity of authors' contracts, the literary agent normally has a law degree from an institution recognized to be a place of learning. (Note: if the author is allergic to lawyers, the author may need to be desensitized before coming into personal contact.)

However, the literary agent is the type of lawyer who likes to take risks — quite rare, and therefore estimable. Your agent may not put in as much time trying to sell your book as you expended in the writing of it, but is less likely to bind you to a contract that includes a clause committing the author to autographing tours into parts of Africa where cannibalism survives as a visitor experience.

As for the agent's commission, this varies from the standard 10 percent of royalties to a higher cut that indicates the agent doesn't anticipate a six-figure sum will be paid for the movie rights to your book of home-cooking recipes.

Dickering with your literary agent is a bad start to the relationship unless the agent insists on a doctor's report on your life expectancy. If you are uncomfortable with the agent's proposed commission (anything over fifty-fifty), it is prudent to abandon the negotiation and consider *self-publication*. Yes, the vanity press is the ultimate ego trip and may cost the author thousands of dollars in printing charges without a commensurate return, but any royalties earned *are entirely yours.* Auto-gratification, yes, but of a sort that you can discuss with your tax accountant.

WRITERS' UNIONS

Next to a Hollywood marriage, a writers' union is the most fragile grouping in the entire labour movement. Why? *Because writers are chronic individualists.* Also, it's a lonely job, and nobody has to do it.

It is possible for a writer to split his allegiance among several different brotherhoods of labour — the Writers' Union, the Screenwriters' Union, the Playwrights' Union, etc. And, as fraternities go, they are all about as Spartan as the flesh can bear. Union members must confine satisfaction to their getting a newsletter that confirms that a member has somehow earned enough to pay for the subscription.

A writers' union never goes on strike. It knows that nobody would notice. Including most of the strikers.

In fact, it is hard to imagine a picket line of militant poets. (The line would have to scan, for one thing.) Outside publishing houses we rarely see a bunch of tough-looking novelists lounging around a barrel of burning wood and brandishing signs: MEDIA UNFAIR TO FICTION.

Publishers know that there is a wealth of scabs out there, writers eager to grab any assignment under the banner of *freelancing* — a roguish term for having the bargaining scruples of the pigeons in Trafalgar Square.

To protest our working conditions, we militant union writers may threaten to hold our breath until we faint, but the employer will simply step over our emaciated bodies.

True, we get some honest satisfaction, as well as central heating, from burning the rejection strips in the stove. But integrity butters no parsnips.

The bottom line: creative writing is a lonely job that nobody asked us to do. We are trying to provide a non-essential service to a public that couldn't care less whether we thrive or merely strive. No one should be surprised, therefore, if the writing career expected to be a bowl of cherries proves to be only the pits.

Meantime, cherish your illusions!

CARE AND FEEDING OF LIBRARIANS

Is there any connection between the disproportionate popularity of female authors' novels and the fact that most public librarians are women?

Certainly not. Perish the thought, Clyde. The only reason librarians order more copies of female-authored novels than those written by guys is that women read more novels than men do. (Here statistics are hard to come by, but if you stand around in a library long enough you will see that most of the borrowers are women. You may also be asked to leave if you are making rude lip noises.)

Anyhow, the suspicion lingers — after a survey of library bookshelves — that for male novelists the odds aren't the only thing stacked against them. So are their books. Of which the library has bought only one copy, shared between a multitude of branches, and with the loan requiring a prescription.

This suspicion is, of course, entirely unwarranted. Library purchases aren't gender-specific but are based on the popularity and track record of the author who, if male, will be smart not only to make a personal appearance at every library branch but also offer to redecorate the washroom, gratis.

The author's relationship with librarians would be much easier to manage if librarians did nothing but stamp books in and out and check the people at the reading table for vital signs. Today, emancipated by the computer, librarians have time to *read* books. They are *knowledgeable*, reading book reviews in journals, instead of minding their own business. An ugly turn of events this, negating the author's personal charm and his offer of marriage in exchange for having his book displayed on the bestseller table.

However, the author/librarian relationship is so vital that the first place that an author should visit, when in another town, is the public library. You introduce yourself, recover quickly when your name fails to ring a bell, and effusively congratulate the staff on their being able to include books in their library.

In short, the public library is your home away from home. If it helps to dub yourself the Loan Ranger, fine. Circulating isn't just for libraries. And as for the Ivory Tower — uh-uh, no takeout.

BOOK PROMOTION

M ay involve public readings. Which, in terms of lip movement, aren't as much fun as French kissing.

Reading to a live — temporarily, at least — audience may not be mentioned in the fine print of your contract with the publisher. But it is tacitly understood that the author is committed to a personal appearance over and above just taking a bow.

Confirmed introverts need not apply.

The shrinking violet is soon compost.

Yes, in most trades the good worker gets a promotion. But in the writing trade the promotion gets *him*. Or her. In severe cases book promotion involves a nationwide tour, with readings in places at unknown distance from the nearest lavatory. Standing with your legs crossed for extended periods can leave you with a permanent hip problem to supplement the chronic twitch in one eye.

True, some authors are extroverted enough to be able to actually *enjoy* reading their work to a live audience. Charles Dickens revelled in it. He also enjoyed acting in amateur theatre. The guy was truly weird. Yet he turned out some pretty good stuff.

However, he never had to promote his book on a local television station — on what is not so much a channel as a ditch — that needs to fill in some time between the morning news and Daffy Duck. This ordeal requires the author to give some attention to personal appearance. Any royalties produced by the interview are cancelled out by the cost of his having to get a haircut.

On the plus side, the TV interview across a table eliminates the author's concern about how he or she looks below the waist. In contrast, a stand-up stint before a live audience entails a dress code that doesn't include the sweatpants and grubby sneakers that are your normal sub-equatorial apparel.

After a public reading, the author will be surrounded by aspiring authors desperate to know the secret of how you managed to get published on the strength of such fragile material. Some may rub your nose for luck. And one or two will confront you with a copy of your new book to be autographed with a dictated message that may be longer than the book itself.

Yes, book promotion is a cross to be borne as cheerfully as possible, body and spirit bowing meekly to trade. As ego trips go, it is one of the less scenic. But it does provide a bit of a change from the constrictive humility that is the corset of our character.

REMUNERATION

The labourer is worthy of his hire.

— Luke 10:7

But if you haven't been hired, you may be out of Luke. In fact, as a freelance writer, you may earn squat.

Independently wealthy: that is the ideal financial condition in which to engage in writing for public consumption. Or, if you enjoy good relations with filthy-rich parents documented to be in poor physical condition: okay, it may be safe for you to engage in writing as a career.

Now, assuming you have written something that a publisher or a film company accepts, what may you expect by way of financial compensation for, possibly, years of toiling over a hot novel?

The proceeds are called *royalties*. These royalties are no relation to what the queen of England earns. Or even her footmen. Unless, that is, you are fortunate enough to produce an international bestseller translated into fifty tongues, including sign language.

Writers' royalties are just a cut above the wages of sin, other than mortal. The usual cut is 10 percent of the take. If you have a literary agent, the cheque goes to your agent, who takes his or her percentage of the percentage. This is why the writer needs to have some elementary knowledge of math, in regard to the dynamics of percentages, to prevent acute disappointment on finding that a cold-blooded science of numbers has reduced his just deserts to thin pickings.

Now some writers — especially poets — profess not to care about a payoff, being so grateful for public exposure that they will face starvation with smiles on their emaciated faces.

These writers are, to put it mildly, *scabs*.

They exacerbate the problem of earning a living for the rest of us who have a meaningful relationship with eating. Yes, it may be tempting to write a freebie article for your church bulletin or community paper, but it can put you on a slippery slope and should never be done under your proper name.

As for those who trespass against this credo, let us remember them in our prayers at the altar of the Almighty Buck!

NEW RELATIONSHIPS

Creative writing is often thought of as a solitary occupation, cribbing the soul and causing skin problems. Not so! The fact is that you will *broaden* your horizon of relationships, all of them with computer repairmen. And this without ever having to go outside your own home. Talk about your modern conveniences!

Yes, this is true intimacy, without (usually) the bother of contraception. You may have secrets from your spouse or lover, but your PC doctor not only has a key to your house but is one of the few persons intimate enough to see you cry.

Unlike modern heart surgery or hip replacement, computer repair is never a quick operation. This is why, as the hours crawl by in your study or office while your computer problem defies diagnosis let alone treatment, you and your computer guy have ample time to settle in, perhaps even set up the light housekeeping needed to accommodate all the accordion folders of analytic discs that your PC will vomit while continuing to obfuscate its problem.

Thus closeted with your computer guy over an extended period of time — an operation performed without anaesthetic except maybe a stiff shot of brandy ("Kiss me, Hardy!") — you babble details of your private life that even your immediate family (those related by blood rather than printer ink) are unaware of.

Note: when you prepare your income tax return you may be tempted to list your computer guy as a dependent, as well as a professional expense. Alas, the Receiver General won't buy it. You will just have to love your computer guy for himself, keeping in mind that you could do worse, hanging out in singles bars.

Should you marry your computer guy? If you are both male, probably not. And even if the patient's owner is female, her husband (Micromed) isn't going to be home much, but closeted in the study of some other woman whose computer isn't the only thing being turned on.

THE FUN FACTOR

Okay, forget about the six-figure royalties, the book-of-the-month award, and guest appearances on *Larry King Live*. Dross, all of it, unless you really *enjoy* writing.

Writing should be the most fun you can have with your fly zipped.

Another test: do you actually relish writing letters to your friends or family or even an editor you have never met? Have you become more aroused by writing a love letter than by being with the person it is addressed to? Yes? Good! You have the divine afflatus.

Granted, in terms of creative satisfaction, writing can never be as fulfilling as working with power tools. No novelist looks as gratified as a good handyman who can create something he may sit on. Comfortably.

Yet, unlike other creative pursuits, with writing a person should feel guilty if he or she does *not* engage in it. The Muse is a draconian mistress, jealous of any attention paid to another paramour, or routine activities like house cleaning or car washing, or indeed just about anything that subjects the mind to the body.

This is why very few notable writers are golfers. Both activities require a high degree of concentration over an extended period. Also, one round of golf could wipe out most writers' yearly income, even without hiring a caddy.

True, there *is* the hazard of becoming *too* addicted to writing, to the exclusion of any diversion except going to the bathroom. (Which should never be seen as a recreation area, the rubber duckie notwithstanding.)

When working on the novel or the play, one should avoid becoming too emotionally involved with a character that one has created. A murder mystery, for instance, loses some of its impact if the author is unable to bring himself to kill at least one of his personae.

Instead, writing should be madness in moderation. The urge, though spontaneous, ought always be yielded to unless one is operating a vehicle or engaged in sexual intercourse. And the thrill of finding *le mot juste*, the resonant phrase, the sentence that wings into new heights of expression — such is the reward for which our life provides no substitute.

Creative writing. *"Ce vice impuni"* — this unpunished vice. Let him who is without sin pick up his pencil and get the lead out!

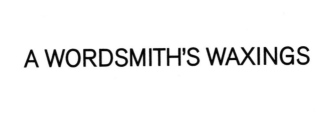

A WORDSMITH'S WAXINGS

A CLASS ACT

I have always enjoyed teaching. It was a power trip rarely afforded writers. And it gave me classes that included female students. I never expected sexual favours in exchange for higher marks. This reduced the potential for disappointment. But only slightly.

I once considered being a Girl Guides counsellor. I wanted to show them how to start a fire without clothing. I was not accepted. Gender discrimination of the worst order. I never got to deliver my urinary warning: the going gets hard when the hard gets going.

I have taught at several levels: standing, sitting, and floor (to demonstrate the dangling participle). As a creative writing instructor, I found that my female students were ready to do almost anything to get an A+. I didn't fail one of them, because none of them failed me. But I found that teaching adult female students is a power trip with dangerous curves.

The girls in my class soon learned that dotting their *i*'s and crossing their *t*'s was not as productive as batting their eyes and crossing their knees. I always left my office door open to encourage them to come in for an interlude. I tried to be fatherly without entirely ruling out incest.

Although some of my female students were openly passionate about raising their grades, none of them sexually assaulted me in my office. I was careful to keep my desk between us. (Note: professors who try to conduct interviews without a desk are asking for trouble that could land them in the Supreme Court.)

Sometimes a female student would wear a provocative perfume that stimulated my most sensitive organ: my nose. Chanel and my nose have never had a good relationship. In fact, the more expensive a scent is, the more likely it is that my nose will make a scene.

I learned the hard way that it is fatal to rehearse your ad libs. To keep students' attention within the city limits, a teacher should have a quick wit. An unpredictable temper will also help hold students' attention, but may cause the teacher to be remembered as Mr. Chips on the Shoulder.

So, what teaching taught *me* was the value of having power over other people *yet not having to use it*. This criterion poses the prerequisite of the teacher's having a *personality*. A teacher with no personality may be less subject to mood change, but has lost his or her advantage over the dictaphone.

I also learned that there was a limit on how far my female students would go to raise their grades. Their grades were all that they were prepared to raise.

My office door was always open for interviews with students having trouble, or looking for it, but all I got was the draft.

I have had to give up teaching because of a bad back. It is hard to lecture effectively from a reclining position. But I do miss the power trip. I can understand why Hitler committed suicide. Once you have held the reins in your hands, you cannot be content with the view from the horse's ass.

A CLEAR-CUT CASE

Meddlesome environmentalists (aka tree-huggers) argue that logging our public forests contributes to the effects of global warming: rising oceans, sinking feelings, wimping of wildlife, etc., that will reduce the quality of life for our grandchildren.

Well, tough titty!

I've never really liked kids, anyhow. I think they are a flawed way of making adults. I certainly don't value a future generation as much as having a nice car parked in my garage. One that can be traded in when it becomes a teenager.

And right now my car is *not* a gas guzzler. It sips. Its emissions are mostly carbon monoxide, which helps to reduce human population growth. *My* family has already stopped growing.

Nor does my car contribute to the deforestation that is blamed for global warming. My car hasn't hit a tree for years, and only a glancing blow when it did. Indeed the problem is not how my car is driven but the fact that a forest is not a rotating crop. It takes five hundred years to mature. Far too long. We need to crossbreed the fir and cedar with some of the weeds in my garden so that they take only days to graduate from forest to lumber yard.

Yes, it is a challenge to produce a rotating crop (forest) that normally takes five hundred years to mature. But we can make a start by replacing the word *clear-cutting* with something that sounds less wholesale. Arborectomy perhaps?

If we can get the green crowd to think of loggers as arborectomists who are also working hard to cross the cedar with the potato to produce a tree that peels easily, people will soon forget the loss of a perch for owls.

Meantime, the environmentalists will keep bitching that logging our forests will reduce the quality of life for our grandchildren. So, our responsibility is clear: *do not have grandchildren.* We have ample evidence that grandchildren are bad for posterity. They emit noxious gases, and once they have developed beyond the larval stage, they become a major cause of damage to a family automobile.

A small grandchild will also — if emitted from the home — pee into a lake or ocean, compromising our more sensitive forms of aquatic life. Including lifeguards.

As for this "global warming" business, I have difficulty believing it. My heating bill gets higher every year. How can this be if the Earth is getting dangerously toasty? Okay, so the Arctic ice is melting so fast the polar bears have nothing to jump off. Tough teddy! We still have ample space for them in zoos.

Okay, so maybe there is some scientific evidence that the oceans are rising. They are still a good distance from my house. When I find a dead mackerel on my porch, yes, then I'm with you, Suzuki. Green around the bank deposit, eh?

A MOMENT OF MAJESTY

My bank now has a doorman. Yes, a genuine flunky who opens the bank door for me even if I'm not carrying a bag of cash for deposit. Although my bank's doorman may not be as dressy as the concierge at the Savoy, the servility is every bit as gratifying to someone like me who has limited access to the haute monde.

Indeed, I may go in and out of the bank several times just to savour the flunky rush. I thank the doorman every time I saunter past him. I don't tip him. It would cheapen our relationship, I feel. But I always say "Thank you!" and try to make eye contact to assure him that, as a devout determinist, I recognize that it is only by the fickleness of fate that I'm not opening the door for him. A brief glimpse of common humanity, this, at Mammon's very portal.

On leaving the bank, I hesitate to ask the doorman to whistle up a cab for me. It would be a moment of grandeur, but I see no whistle on his uniform. And whistling may not be part of his job description.

More sobering is the thought that the doorman doubles as a security person in disguise. The bank is trying to avoid alarming customers with such evidence that a gang of robbers may burst into the bank at any time and shoot anyone who resists losing his place in line for a teller. Like, me.

Already my bank has a sign above the tellers: CUSTOMERS ARE REQUESTED TO REMOVE THEIR HATS AND SUNGLASSES.

I rarely wear a hat, or sunglasses, especially in the bank, so I'm already failing to comply with the injunction. I consider this to be a safer option than trying to hold my hat in my mouth while my hands are occupied with the teller.

For a while I viewed my bank's doorman as a status symbol, but I notice that branches of other banks are also installing doormen. Bank doormen are a growth industry in this prosperous land of ours. Our medicare system is going to be severely taxed by the plague of doorman's elbow, a bursitis caused by competitive banking.

Meantime, the proliferation of bank doormen is a sad commentary on the failure of the automatic door. Which, of course, is supposed to sense a person's approach and open just long enough to catch the entrant in the crotch. The automatic door has worked well for the drugstore, which has enjoyed a boost in sales of Band-Aid and other emergency treatments for victims of door assaults.

Which evokes the question: Now that all the competing banks have a doorman, what will be their next stratagem to seduce depositors? Maybe a complimentary shoe shine? Or all-female tellers dressed like Hooters servers to draw interest at a higher rate than government bonds?

Okay, so maybe I'm overly sensitive to changes in Western society that may fuel the terrorism of the Taliban and other picky

cults. But I'm braced for the day when my bank's doorman is backed by a bevy of dancing girls garbed to affect my interest rate. Then I'm outta there. Back to the piggy bank!

A NOCTURNAL EMISSION

It has been alleged that I snore in my sleep. A cruel canard. This is demeaning and destructive to my self-image as an icon. I believe that I am close enough to my nose to be aware if I am snoring. And I haven't heard a sound. Truly. Naturally, we all deny that we snore. It is so beastly. The most that I will admit to is heavy nocturnal breathing with some seismic side effects.

"Sure," says some smart aleck, "you haven't heard your snore because you were asleep at the time." Nonsense! I am a light sleeper, weighing only a hundred and fifty pounds on my home scales, which I trust more than the hysterical device in my doctor's office.

"To sleep, perchance to dream," moans Hamlet, who should have added "perchance to snore." The nose is the second most likely organ to get us into trouble. It is clearly implicated in snoring. Which is defined by Webster — who may have ruined a relationship himself — as "a snorting or grunting sound." Now, that is obviously disgusting. Unseemly for a gentleman, a relationship liability for a lady.

People spend big bucks to lower their snore. It is more practical, for me at least, to admit to *apnea*, i.e., temporary cessation of breathing. This sometimes happens when I put a pillow over my face to muffle the chirping of oversexed robins outside my bedroom window. I identify with worms. Burrow a lot.

Anyhow, my snore volume is modulated by whether I sleep on my back, stomach, or some combination induced by income tax. My shortage of nightmares gives me concern about my subconscious. Has the sub sunk? Surely I must have committed enough sins — of omission, if not cardinal — to find utterance in turbulent snoring? Yet nothing has registered on the Richter scale.

It may be that my nose is too tired to snore, having had to deal with my hay fever all day. Despite the name, this fever is not entirely dependent on hay. Anything airborne, smaller than a Boeing 707, will agitate my nostrils into a frenzy.

I recognize that my nose is one of the most commonly compromised organs of modern man. But I don't want my nose to get a swelled head.

Anyhow, snoring is one of the lesser evils of falling asleep at the wheel. Of a moving vehicle, that is.

In any event, I have found that the best way to muffle the snores that are reputed to agitate small objects on shelves, and be held responsible for the FOR SALE sign on the house nearest my bedroom, is to install an electric fan. The fan produces an oscillating uproar that is a big disappointment for mosquitoes misled by an open window.

A guy will work double overtime, get a second job, rob a bank, whatever, just to pay for separate bedrooms in the matrimonial home that will accommodate the moonlight sonata rendered by his conk.

There is now, I understand, a medical operation that alleviates snoring without removing the nose. Nobody has the operation. Operating rooms stand empty, waiting for noses that never come in.

My wife's remedy for my snoring: sleeping with earplugs. This puts the responsibility on me to panic in event of burglars. None has ventured in. I presume that my snores have a menacing quality that deters any intruder with normal hearing.

A PICKLE AT THE PUMP

The secret to growing old gracefully is to minimize those activities that involve getting out of bed. (You can also make a fool of yourself *in* bed, but there is less chance of your activities being witnessed by a crowd.)

This is why, when it comes time to refill the gas tank of my frugal little auto, I seek the station with the fewest observers. That often means paying more per gallon, but I see it as the best chance of avoiding any incidents that provide amusement for other customers. And cause station operators to age visibly. (I have observed one of them crossing himself as I edged jerkily toward his pump island.)

I aim at self-service pumps because the last time I used full service I scared the attendant by releasing the brake instead of opening the hood. (Those station attendants have inordinately high expectations about the elderly driver, just because he is sitting behind the steering wheel.)

Anyhow, on this latest intercourse with a gas pump, I was right away flummoxed by the different grades of gas. Class distinction, leaded. As months had passed since my last encounter with a pump, I had forgotten what grade of gas I had bought, or whether the gas had any grade beyond elementary. So, on impulse, I pushed the buttons for *all* the grades, glad to see that this had caused the pump no visible trauma.

However, as I stood holding the hose expectantly, I was disturbed to see that I had forgotten to open my gas tank flap. Now, I have enough marbles left to know that if the gas tank is not accessible, filling the tank becomes much more complicated — if not impossible. So, in full panic mode, I clawed at the flap before recalling that the release gismo was *inside the car*. Somewhere. Scrambling back into the front seat, and still gripping the hose lest it start gushing the makings of a raging inferno, I yarded on the lever that opened the trunk. *Close* to the gas tank flap, but no cigar.

Now flailing around in full panic mode, I managed to turn on the radio at a time when music hath not enough charm to soothe the agitated breast. But it did help to create a carnival atmosphere while the union of hose and gas tank was consummated.

The gush of gas into, hopefully, the tank was so violent that I immediately aborted the emission — *coitus interruptus*, plus tax.

Now, some people — real guys, hair on their chest, etc. — are cool enough to be able to pump gas and watch the fuel gauge at the same time. Me, I have to concentrate on one area or the other. I am nothing if not focused. But this rigidity — with its passing resemblance to rigor mortis — does seem to exasperate other customers waiting to use the pump. And noticing them waiting tight-lipped in the queue creates, for me, a pressure I would have preferred to have got in my tires.

Thus I abort the emission. Tank unfulfilled. And hastily move the car to the station's Siberia. And I do not surprise the station attendant when I drop my credit card on the floor. He has doubtless witnessed the whole episode of my gas purchase, and seems surprised when the card works.

Does this total ineptitude in gassing my car bother me? Not really. No one has ever been seriously hurt. And I continue to think of myself as an absent-minded professor with no class.

A SAMPLER OF EVIL SPIRITS

After cheap gin, these are the worst kind of spirits to have in the house. They affect mostly old guys. Young guys have bad luck, old guys, *goblins*.

The Fly Zipper. This miscreant, skulking in a senior's pants, insidiously relieves itself — zip! — at the least appropriate moment, i.e., when the victim is taking communion, taking a bus, or taking it for granted that people are smiling because they find him witty. When actually he is in a zippidy-do-do.

The insidious fly zipper is sexist, women's dress closures being relatively benign, even gainfully employed, in a pant suit. But when striking during a job interview, the fly zipper can total a guy's chance of employment.

Equally hazardous, **Serpentine Shoelaces**. Deadly, these are, when working in cahoots with a bad back. It is all too easy for arthritic fingers to become hopelessly compromised by an involvement with a serpentine shoelace, even when the tab is not venomous.

Another bane of the balding, **Shrinking Briefs**. A person first notices this phenomenon when too many of his waking hours are spent trying to pull his briefs up over his butt. Mount Burger. Could *we* have put on those pounds? No weigh! Blame cheap foreign labour! It is creating more pork chops than nature intended. Hence our waiting for hips that never come in.

And we may be tempted to indulge in *exercise*. Physical exercise can be harmful to your health unless used with caution. Hazards include:

The Barbell. Dropped on your toe, this weight can immobilize you for longer than is compatible with your job description.

The Stationary Bike. Extended periods in the saddle may render a man sexually impotent. The lone cowboy was paying the price. As for riding a *mobile* bike, this involves *hills*. Which can supplement your outing with a trip to emergency. Other static threats:

The Parking Meter. If it is having a bad day — dogs peeing on it, horses hitched to it, etc. — the parking meter will balk at taking any coin minted in the known world. It is also in collusion with the street gutter, down which your rejected coin will scuttle, never to be seen again by human eye but helping to finance new subdivisions of hell.

The *underground* parking meter should be ignored entirely. Paying the fine is preferable to the wear and tear on your nervous system caused by forgetting where your car is parked right after you parked it. This is why the parking lot attendant is trained to deal with hysteria.

The Web. The name alone should be warning enough, yet millions of otherwise decent people daily venture into the Web, that sticky lair of the licentious. Here lurks temptation! Shady ladies who once had to traipse the streets to attract customers can now set up a website.

What draws us to the Web? The Apple! Thus does the computer — Satan's late-model temptation — challenge any moral fibre we have left after consorting with our income tax return.

The Spring-Mounted Toilet Seat. This ejection seat should be used only in an emergency. After informing next of kin of your flight plan.

A STICKY WICKET

Why I may henceforth be doing all my banking online, even at the risk of blundering into a porn channel and needing to withdraw my life savings to pay to have my computer neutered:

My visit to the local branch of my bank started innocently enough. The bank's security person even opened the door for me to enter, recognizing me as too venerable to attempt a bank heist. No great shakes, as compliments go, but graciously received.

In fact, we have had so many bank robberies lately in this town that I half expected some large person to pat me down for hidden weapons. Better than having no sex life at all, maybe, but I'm ticklish.

All I really wanted was to fulfill my mission: withdrawing fifty dollars cash from my account without bloodshed.

Walking at normal pace toward my objective, I got a glimpse of myself in the security monitor. Aside from it being too late for me to zip my fly, I appeared to be blending with the crowd okay.

It was not till I was leaning on my cane in the teller's queue that I noticed the sign above her wicket: FOR SECURITY REASONS WE ASK THAT YOU REMOVE YOUR HAT AND SUNGLASSES. THANK YOU.

Now it just so happened that I was wearing my hat and sunglasses. Why, I don't remember. It was neither raining nor sunny out. Perhaps it was to compensate for the incipient bald spot. Anyhow, I didn't panic. I understood that stripping my head was necessary to enable the surveillance camera to record my identity and make it easier for a prosecutor to gain my conviction. But I am fearful of any kind of photograph because I register as guilty even when I haven't done anything.

I hastily removed the hat — a grubby old slouch with a graffito: CANADIAN WILDLIFE FEDERATION. A bank is no place to be pushing wildlife. In my haste to remove the wild hat, I knocked the sunglasses off my nose. This affected my vision, temporarily, so that in hastily bending to retrieve them, I molested the lady ahead of me in the queue. With both the glasses and the hat on the floor, I now had the attention of pretty well everyone in the bank except the manager, who has a private office.

The lady ahead of me was gracious about my feeling her up and, in fact, picked up my wallet — which had seized the opportunity to escape my jacket pocket — and handed it to me with a nice smile. Which may have been related to her seeing me try to stuff my hat into my jacket pocket and stick my sunglasses in my wallet while holding my cane in my mouth.

Haggard, at last at the teller's wicket, I was greeted by a smiling young woman who must have observed the gimpy striptease. She said, "You can leave your hat on, sir."

"Really?" The inference was that, even if he pulled a gun, this geezer would never reach the door before being tackled by somebody's grandmother.

"Thank you." I now had at least one hand free to get into trouble.

"What," asked the teller, "can I do for you?"

Good question. In the emotional upheaval of reaching the teller's wicket, my mind had gone blank with regard to original motivation. "Will you marry me?" was my initial choice as response, fortunately discarded. Instead I said, "I need to take out some money."

The teller's smile vanished.

"I'm sorry," I said. I had already created enough disturbance in this respectable house of usury without my aggravating the nuisance by demanding money — albeit my money. They might have to open a huge safe someplace just to extract fifty bucks because this geezer can't be trusted with a credit card.

It occurred to me that I was reliving Stephen Leacock's interlude with a bank in which he deposited a cheque to his account, then decided he needed some cash. When the teller asked him how much he wanted to take out, the flustered Leacock replied, "All of it."

"I need fifty dollars," I told the teller, "in twenties."

She didn't bat an eye. Our relationship had matured quickly, it seemed, as she doled out two twenties and a ten. I offered no resistance. Instead I just put the bills under my hat, picked up my cane and glasses, and marched resolutely to the door I had made the mistake of entering.

The security guard opened the door for me, standing well clear and on the alert. I marched through with the resolute step of the person who has survived a hostile environment rife with opportunity to make a damn fool of himself, emerging mission accomplished.

The bottom line: there is nothing like extracting money from the bank, to make you really love your credit card.

ABOUT YOUR SOX LIFE

Okay, guys, answer me this: When you get a hole in one of your socks, do you:

(a) darn the sock?

(b) damn the sock?

(c) discard the breached sock but save the remaining sock for pairing with another sole survivor sock of similar colour?

(d) throw away both socks, because Christmas is coming and with it a plethora of gift socks, some of which may be worn in public?

(e) just wear the holed sock and try to think of it as pedal ventilation?

This is a problem that affects mostly men. As I understand it — and here I must confess to having done little personal research — when a woman gets a hole in her pantyhose, the whole garment self-destructs, a soundless explosion that explains why women wear slacks. It's a writeoff.

A woman then buys a whole new pair of nylons, after saving the unexploded stocking to strain fruit juice. (Such treated juice may be mildly intoxicating to guys who don't need much excuse for attempted sexual assault.)

Guys also face the dilemma of whether or not to try to resuscitate a ruptured sock. Those of us who have seen military service will have been issued a "housewife," a khaki pouch fully armed with needles and enough thread to strangle the raw recruit. The veteran may be tempted to resort to this dangerous souvenir of war, trying to repair a ravaged sock and learning, painfully, that he no longer has the hand-eye coordination required to thread a needle without drawing more blood than he can afford to lose.

To summarize: "mending" a holed sock is an operation that should be left to an experienced surgeon. The same way that cutting the offending toenail should have been left to a very experienced sawyer. It has been said that "it's never too late to learn." WRONG. Our head is too far from our feet to ever understand fully what mischief they have got up to.

Also, there is evidence that a man who mends his own sock — especially while sitting in a rocking chair — can induce male menopause years before his libido's normal expiry date. That is why it is sensible to use the ruptured sock only to wrap an outside tap for winter, and then set forth to the nearest men's clothing store *for the express purpose of buying a new pair of socks.* Or, if you have faith in your longevity, *two* pairs of socks.

If, dear reader, you are a woman who suspects that the only reason your boyfriend has shown no wish to go to bed with you is that he is reluctant to remove his shoes and thus expose a ruptured sock and bumptious big toe, make him a present of new socks. No need to knit them yourself. Just get him into a cotton contraceptive that will prevent passion from shredding a sheet.

After all, it's the thought that counts.

ANALYSIS OF KNEE TRANSPOSITION

Do you cross your knees? If so, why? What is your motivation in placing one leg astride the other? Have you ever thought about this as being possibly a defence mechanism, a basic contraceptive? Or is your suspending one leg over the other a considered relocation of a limb, rather than just an instinctive response to a threat to your lap? Perhaps a surrogate chastity belt?

I ask these trenchant questions as a person — male, which may be relevant — who rarely crosses his knees. Whether alone or in company. One reason for this may be that I am of a stocky build, lacking the abnormally long legs that facilitate their transposition. (Some women are lanky enough to be able to lock one foot around the opposite ankle — nature's way of discouraging rape.)

From a lifetime of careful observation of the leg-crossing phenomenon, I have concluded that some women — mostly pre-menopausal — not only cross but actually *swing* the crossed leg as an attention-getting device. More often, however, the crossed-leg swing is an indicator of impatience, a sign that many men have misread at the cost of being hospitalized. By a spike heel to the groin.

For this reason men will be wise to question a woman's crossed knees as an invitation to sexual intercourse, instead relying on more overt signals, such as her emitting a provocative perfume (other than aftershave) or dropping a handkerchief or making kissy noises. (Note: eye-winking may only be spastic.)

Being short of shank, I cross my knees only for the medical test of what's left of my reflexes. By a hammer blow south of the kneecap. This percussion causes the lower part of my leg to swing upward, involuntarily, with enough force to do serious damage to the groin of the doctor slow on his feet.

In all other social situations, however, I sit with both feet firmly planted on the floor, creating a lap that, I'm sure, my secretary would find irresistible, if I had a secretary.

This demure posture, knees uncrossed, costs me the chance to show off my socks. My observation has been that women are easily seduced by argyle. Worn by guys whose only connection with the auld country is their buying cheap Scotch. Bad cess to 'em, I say, without being too clear what it means.

Anyhow, I comfort myself with the thought: the long-legged guy sitting with his knees crossed is merely contending with his need to go to the bathroom. Why would I envy a person with weak kidneys?

Yes, the way I sit indicates complete confidence in my waterworks. This should be an attraction for any woman looking for a mate who requires less laundry to do. But obviously it isn't. Instead they fall in love with some India-rubber guy who can talk with his knees crossed.

However, we all have our cross to bear. And we carry it onto the bus, where crossing his long legs can get the show-off into a peck of trouble. As consolations go, it's no hell, Shorty. But I bet that you're more fun at a party.

ANATOMY OF THE MEDICAL CLINIC

For doctors the medical clinic represents an exciting advance against the pain of paying office rent. Instead of having to fork out for separate premises, a number of physicians and surgeons cluster on one floor of a multi-storey building in any neighbourhood but the patients'.

The medical clinic eliminates the need to make house calls, as the patient can't afford to have a house. Eat your heart out, Hippocrates!

For many taxi companies, the medical clinic — being remote from the patient's home — is the main source of revenue. Chronically ill seniors may well have their most intimate relationship with a Yellow Cab driver.

Those that elect to drive their own vehicles to the medical clinic inevitably find themselves groping through the dark of an underground parking lot, thus compromising the accuracy of any subsequent blood-pressure reading. Here the patient learns that his appointment should have been with an oculist, not the dermatologist.

For the patient who survives the parking lot, the next phase is an elevator ride up to the floor containing the relevant physicians. The elevator provides the patient with close, if not intimate, contact with other persons exhaling highly contagious diseases. Climbing the stairs — on hands and knees, if necessary — may be indicated, unless the patient can avoid inhaling for at least five minutes.

Disgorged at the floor that your doctor's office is reputed to be on, you have your choice of the sofas and chairs designed to make your wait for the doctor to be the experience of a lifetime. You report your arrival to the doctor's securely boothed secretary. Who may or may not make the sign of the cross after ticking off your name on the appointments ledger.

"We will call you when the doctor is ready for you," she says with a straight face. "Please take a seat."

This is the most critical phase of the visit to the medical clinic.

Choosing a seat that allows you to stare at the doctor's secretary will not expedite your admission. As the hours crawl by, what you do is imagine that your doctor is dealing with a patient who has turned violent after being informed he has to give up smoking. Or that he has contracted the clap.

On the table is the inevitable copy of the December 1938 edition of *Reader's Digest* — a rich source of viruses deposited by previous patients. **Do not touch any reading matter at a medical clinic.** Also, pretend to be comatose to avoid conversing with another waiting patient. He may have measles.

If you are accompanied by children in this staging area, you will have a unique opportunity to watch them grow up, start shaving (take a razor), develop breasts, possibly reach maturity, and have children of their own ("Can we go home now, Grandpa?").

You are summoned by loudspeaker — in case someone out of town is not aware of your tryst with the rectal exam. You are now in the corridor leading — in theory at least — to your doctor's examining room. It doesn't matter how recently your doctor has examined you. He is going to examine you again. This can be particularly arduous if you go into the wrong doctor's office. The proctologist's, for example, when you have a foot problem.

In your doctor's office, you find two hard-backed chairs and a sink stained with blood. But no doctor. That busy personage arrives only when assured that you are serious about treatment. He then ignores you, preferring to trust your file. This is why *it is essential to have a healthy file.*

Your doctor soon has you back in the parking lot, clutching a prescription, trying to find your car. If you *do* find your car, you will immediately feel better. Thanks to the medical clinic.

ANDY IS HANDY

Ithink of God as the ultimate handyman. Conversely, I think of my own handyman as the supreme being in our neighbourhood. I worship the ground he brings into the house, on the few occasions when he forgets to remove his sturdy boots.

I make offerings to my handyman — coffee ... tea ... consecrated cookies — to complement the resonant cheque I write for him, after his latest act of salvation for our aging domicile.

Me, I'm not handy. Except in the sense of being readily available, albeit inept. I would make house calls, but it seems that few people have need of a professional writer, even though I will take off my shoes before typing your essay.

This costs me a lot of income, but the ugly fact is I don't understand any tool except the hammer. And have only a marginal grasp on that implement.

But Andy, ah! There is a man who has mastered a whole range of tools and trades: plumber, carpenter, painter, electrician, roofer — you name it, and Andy will refuse to panic at its leaking, smoking, clanking, or otherwise suggesting a problem I can't solve with Scotch tape.

This is why Andy's heads my list of emergency phone numbers, right up there with 911 and the pharmacy.

The fly in this ointment is that Andy is in such high demand in a neighbourhood of white-collar nerds like me that he really needs to be booked before the front door falls off or the clothesline suffers a hernia. Also, because money is no object when your fence has just collapsed, Andy can afford to take frequent vacations in the West Indies. I have never been able to afford the West Indies myself, but visit them vicariously while serving Andy his post-op coffee and cookies. Those native girls on the beach, wow!

When Andy recounts these earthly rewards of his calling, I have to question the value of special training. The jack of all trades would appear to trump my M.A. Or writing as a profession. No one phones me pleading for help to repair a split infinitive. Or prune a dangling participle. I am expendable. Andy is an essential service.

My previous handyman, Fred, had a wealthy East Indian client who, on vacation, took Fred to India with him, all expenses paid, so that Fred could meet a maharajah uncle, who was having a problem with his elephant. Fred fixed the elephant — probably with a new washer — earning several subsequent trips to India, just for fun.

Here we find the only prerequisite for being a handyman: he has to be single. I have never met a handyman who had a wife, or even a full-time mistress. No woman would put up with living with a handyman, I reckon, because the phone is always ringing — for him — while the repairs needing done at her home remain unattended to.

Thus handyman is a sort of monkish trade. Where is it taught? I know of no educational institution that has a Handyman Department. So it's like the sex trade: there is more money to be made outside formal education facilities.

Yes, I cherish Andy. (Not his real name. I don't want competition for his succour.) I don't know what I would do without my handyman par excellence. And I'll be calling him as soon as he's back from the Bahamas.

ANTIQUE CAR DRIVING

Driving my car at an age I couldn't avoid without bloodshed, I find that the safest time to exit the garage is when I have good reason to believe there will be no other cars on the road. This can mean a departure time of 5:00 a.m. just to go to Safeway. Whose staff assume I am part of their security system. I wear dark glasses rain or shine.

When applying for my driver's licence renewal, I resent being asked for proof of age. Hell, the inquisitor in the cage just has to look at me to see that I am no spring chicken. But, oh, no, she pushes back the bribe that I have taken some trouble to include in my documentation. Integrity? I hate to believe it. Those Nosy Parkers are just overpaid in my view.

If on the road, by some nasty stroke of fate, I see a vehicle in my rearview mirror, I immediately pull over to the curb to facilitate my being overtaken. Is the overtaker grateful for this concession? Not a whit. More likely he scowls at losing an opportunity to intimidate someone, having blown it with his wife.

Thus I believe that there ought to be a hand signal that says "Please excuse my being. Devoted to crawling." My simply waving my hand out the window is too readily read as an obscene gesture. Aggravating the situation.

For some guys, highway driving offers the test of manhood once provided by the jousting match. So, do they regard my deferring to their passage as a courtly gesture? No, they do not. They sneer at a senior anal emission, or old fart. I return their greeting by uplifting the two-finger sign of rectal intrusion. Vee for vermin.

My car is not a classic model of anything except the inability to afford something better. I never drive it to a first-class restaurant, in case they refuse to serve me. I try to avoid parking on a downtown street, because panhandlers ignore me as a bum *manqué*. When I take the car in for servicing, the mechanics sidle up to make buying offers that can only make my car feel worse "*Sshh*," I say. "This car has a very sensitive carburetor."

I hesitate to let anyone else drive my car, except a trained mechanic able to deal with automotive neuroses. Among which is the lamentable tendency of the windshield wipers being activated, not to say hysterical, just because I am trying to change gear. The frantic wipers can make other drivers put their hands out their windows to confirm precipitation. Accidents result. And I hate it when those occur. So I now let my wife do most of the driving, as a token of my devotion to living. This would affect my manhood, if I had any left. Luckily for me, I left it behind somewhere in male menopause. Probably during a trip to Ottawa.

Anyhow, I don't hear the call of the open road as well as I once did. I can't say that I really miss having other drivers honking at me. Nor do I rankle because younger members of my family refer to my car as "the chicken coupe." I do have other sources of chagrin, believe me!

To sum up: as an automobile owner, I have an excellent safety record, based on letting someone else do the driving. Only way to go!

CAUSE FOR ALARM

L ove thy neighbour. Or at least try to stay on speaking terms with the creep. Reason: you may need help in an emergency. Especially if you live in the city (the scene of most urban crime).

You also need to subscribe to an alarm system. Which consists of a control panel on a wall some distance away from the furnace control. (Just turning up the heat will not deter a really determined intruder.)

Your electronic alarm system is such that pressing the wrong button will get your house immediately surrounded by police. Who may or may not lob a grenade through a window, if alcohol has affected your choice of alarm buttons. Much then depends — if the paddy wagon is not your first choice of transportation — on whether you have shaved recently or are a very old lady or both.

The problem — for me at least — is that panic can set in on very short notice, causing me to forget the code for turning off the vociferous alarm. Printing the code on my wrist means my delaying taking a bath and subsequent divorce proceedings.

This drill becomes ineffective if, for some reason, I leave the house. Then I must depend on at least three (3) neighbours, to whom I have given a front door key, so that they can provide the police with access without calling in a bulldozer. These neighbours will need to know the alarm turnoff code plus a password, like *eureka*, plus how to turn off the alarm with their bare hands.

These are requirements that no neighbour in his right mind would assume. To overcome key-holder resistance, therefore, it will be necessary for you to include compensation, such as your virginity if you are female, or a lifetime subscription to *Playboy*. Each of these neighbours is issued with:

(a) your house key

(b) the code to shut off your alarm in their lifetime

(c) data for police to reach you, unless you have left the country

(d) the gift bottle of non-local wine

If none of your neighbours have given you the key and alarm code for *their* house. you have solid evidence that they:

(a) don't trust you with access to their furniture, or

(b) suspect that you will use their bathroom, or

(c) prefer to keep the relationship at arm's length, or farther.

Because reciprocity rules, you will be given custody of neighbours' keys, along with the vital password for each. You will lose these at once.

Besides having your key, each neighbour must know your alarm's password. This password will also be on file with your security provider, who lives on a planet some distance from your house. The password should be brief (a monosyllable) without being obscene, profane, or easy to guess. The alarm may also be silenced with a single shot to the battery.

Note: if you are avoiding firearms because of the temptation to shoot yourself, you probably aren't ready for an alarm system.

AS I RECALL

There is a remedy, I believe, for short-term memory loss, but I forget what it is. It may come to me. I welcome any reminder except tax notices.

I do remember that my memory is not reliable for events happening earlier than five minutes ago. Yet I can remember clearly things that may not have happened at all. It evens out.

Tying a string around my finger to remind me of something has proved to be ineffective. I forget what the string is for, and I may require assistance getting the string off. (Gnawing string can be time-consuming.)

Now, to be an absent-minded professor has a certain panache. Nobody expects him to zip his fly. But I don't have my Ph.D. An M.A. doesn't hack it.

I once tried a high-fibre diet reputed to improve short-term memory. But it just made me remember to go to the bathroom.

Currently, having resigned myself to being memory-delinquent about names, I call everyone "Sweetie." Not our garbage pickup guy, of course, but most other folk recognize that they are dealing with a fogey whose marbles have been lost in significant number.

About critical family matters I try to be of two minds, since only one of them is likely to be working. I trust that I am displaying temperate judgment. The fact may be that I have forgotten was the problem is. I scratch my chin, pensively, as if truth were to be found in the stubble.

I have informed family and friends that I am heavily involved in Eastern modes of meditation. What sounds like snoring, to the uninformed, is, in fact, a nasal emission of exhaust from my subconscious.

To compensate for the delinquent memory function, I write reminder notes to myself. Sometimes one of these notes will get mixed up with other missives, so that the milkman gets the reminder to take a laxative, while I read a note asking me to deliver skimmed.

Needless to say — especially if I have already said it — I no longer go to parties that include persons whose names I should know. Especially if we are related by marriage. Luckily, I'm not invited. This saves everyone embarrassment and me taxi fares.

For my frequent visits to doctors' offices, I first make a list of the reasons — usually related to a physical condition — why I am in the doctor's office. (I can easily become flummoxed by the excitement of dropping my pants.) Especially if it is an oculist I am seeing, the pants dropping is an eventuality I should dismiss from mind.

I am not writing my memoirs, because I suspect that I have already written them. They may even have been published. No point in reminding a publisher of his mistake.

On the plus side, if I am carrying a grudge, I forget it before it can develop into *rankling*, that awful condition that can affect one's appetite.

So, I don't wander down Memory Lane, as I suspect that I shall step in a puddle of past foolishness. Let sleeping dogs lie, I tell my memory, unless they have been spayed.

BETTER SAFE THAN SORRY

It's an age-old question: should a guy on a date carry a condom in his wallet, in case he gets lucky, or must he be prepared to complement his wardrobe with a paternity suit? Tailored to beggar him for life.

Having to borrow the prophylactic device from your lady friend smacks of a lack of preparation, as promoted by the Boy Scouts of America and other places.

On the other hand, being able to produce a condom instantly, like a magician plucking a coin out of his nose, may be seen as assumptive, if not plain rude.

Proper timing is critical. Take too long (anything over twenty minutes), and the romantic moment may be lost. Along with your date.

To avoid panic in this critical situation, some guys take the precaution of applying the sheath before making love. Counterproductive, of course, unless you and your bladder are on the same page.

You don't want your safe to go off half-cocked.

Now, what is the protocol if the parties are both guys? Emily Post has never set policy in this situation, and your auto manual is no help, either.

Today's liberated woman is quite apt to carry a condom in her purse to supplement her other auto insurance. In fact, it may be what she carries instead of money. In any case, it is a convenience that her escort should accept graciously, despite the implication that, whatever his hopes to the contrary, he is not seducing a virgin. If this affects his ability to perform, he should seek psychiatric counsel as soon as he can zip his fly.

Should a guy always carry a supply of condoms in his sports jacket? This depends on how often he takes the jacket to the cleaner's without checking the pockets. The female staff will enjoy returning the safes to him in full view of other customers and his parish priest.

Where does a guy obtain a supply of safes? Despite the name, Safeway doesn't carry them. Yes, the liquor store would seem to be a natural marketplace for condoms, but the law fails to recognize the relationship.

Thus the only resort is the drugstore. Whose staff is almost entirely women. Including the cashier. Who is recovering from a bad relationship with a sexual pervert and will ring you up with a look that would curdle turps.

To bypass the pharmacy experience, a guy may practise *coitus interruptus*. And, God knows, he needs practice. Reason: *coitus interruptus* — which is Latin for "Oops, too late!" — requires not only exquisite timing (a factor that eliminates having wine with dinner), but some kind of musical accompaniment to mask any heavy breathing, creaking of joints, or, of course, awkward silence.

This is why a car radio is almost as important an accessory as a mitt for your member. Your humming a tune during intercourse is not going to hack it.

Everything considered, it may be simplest to convert to a faith that proscribes fornication. If you are not sure what fornication means — congratulations! You have jumped the first hurdle on a one-track mind.

CANADA'S GREY EMINENCE

Who is the Receiver General of Canada? Has anyone ever seen him? Or her? It?

Is the Receiver General a general who receives, or a receiver in general? Nobody seems to know. No officer is more private than this general.

Does the Receiver General wear a uniform? Maybe something styled after that of General Rommel, with a row of ribbons for medals awarded by the government in recognition of his wiping out thousands of taxpayers, charging them single-handed?

Yet our Receiver General, unlike generals such as Patton and Montgomery, is self-effacing. Profiles are not kept any lower than the one this general keeps.

Mine is not an idle curiosity, regarding the identity of this highly rank officer. At least once a year I make out a cheque "To the Receiver General," without any further ID. I also now pay a tax accountant, who admits, under questioning, that he, too, doesn't have the foggiest about the identity of this supreme being. Other than that his or her Olympus is located in Ottawa.

Obviously, the Receiver General is not elected to office by popular vote. Or even by *un*popular vote. No matter what he does, the receiver is off the hook. Answering to no one but God. And by appointment only.

Yet the job must be a bit frustrating: to receive all those billions of income tax dollars rolling into his account every April, yet not be able to keep it because the government lays the sleeve on him. Sneaky. The Receiver General's wife must become suspicious, seeing the big bucks moving out of their joint account.

"Oh, sorry, dear. The darn government made me turn a couple of billion over to them. They say they need it so the defence department can buy a new helicopter."

A grim business. All that I personally know about the Receiver General is that he commands Revenue Canada. That doesn't help a lot, because nobody knows much about Revenue Canada either, except that it hibernates all winter, then wakes up in April, hungry as a bear and much more likely to take a bite out of our assets.

My relationship with Revenue Canada, such as it is (rather one-sided), was blighted the year that it informed me, quite coldly, that I was being audited. I learned that a Revenue Canada audition is much less fun than an audition for a show on Broadway. In fact, I got a taste of how it felt to be a heretic in the middle of the Spanish Inquisition. It was impressed upon me that it doesn't pay to diddle Revenue Canada, even at arm's length.

I now understand fully that the Receiver General uses Revenue Canada to impress upon us that it is more blessed to give than to receive. In this respect the Receiver General is less blessed than, say, a general in the Salvation Army.

All of which leads me to suspect that *the Receiver General is not a human person at all*. But the mother of all computers. Secluded in the most secure bunker in Ottawa. And guarded night and day by financial eunuchs.

If this is indeed Revenue Canada's *cordon sanitaire*, there is probably no point in sticking pins in the voodoo doll I made. To err is human, but to forgive is not in the Receiver General's job description. His or her or its response to error is as pitiless as an Aztec priest sacrificing innocent children. In that Ottawa temple, the bowels of compassion haven't had a movement in years.

The bottom line: I've abandoned hope of having a personal relationship with the Receiver General of Canada. I've assigned my tax return prep to an accountant who knows how to placate the god.

I shall miss performing one of the older rites of spring. But I still have a warm rapport with the Easter Bunny.

CHARLES THE WHAT?

Let's face it: chances are, one day Prince Charles will become Canada's monarch. *King* Charles. Not King Charley, let alone King Chuck. Charles. Easier to pronounce (Sharl) in Quebec than is Elizabeth. But *what will be his number?* Charles the What?

Our present queen — and long may she wave! — is, of course, Elizabeth II. There has been only one previous Elizabeth on the throne: Big Betty. Who took the wind out of the sails of the Spanish Armada simply by standing on Dover beach and inhaling.

This was a tough act for any subsequent Liz to follow, Taylor notwithstanding. But Europe's history is cluttered with monarchs dubbed Charles. "Charles" has been the most popular moniker for rulers of France, Sweden, Spain, and any other country where people had trouble remembering names. "Charles" has been right up there with "Louis" as *the* royal handle.

Thus our current Prince Charles is a nominal successor to Charlemagne (Charles the Great), whose field for conquest was somewhat larger than his mistress's tampon.

"O! that I were a glove upon that hand / That I might touch that cheek!" Romeo never got beyond Juliet's more visible accessories in *his* eulogy. Charles the Pioneer.

Other Charleses, presenting less of a challenge to Camilla's hubby, have been Charles the Lame, Charles the Bold, and Charles the Fat. Charles the Mentally Challenged? Possibly. Whatever, our mother country has already had a King Charles I. Seventeenth century. He got beheaded. Too much messing with Scots and Picts, plus budget problems. He was succeeded by Charles II, who made a career of dissolving Parliament, regardless of whether Parliament was into dissolution. He was part of the Restoration period, which had a sexual licence that let the English do anything they wanted, as long as it didn't spook the horses.

Charles II had no legitimate children, so it seems safe to assume that our next monarch will be Charles III. Whose image will one day grace Canadian currency. This may enhance the value of the American dollar.

But Canada will not also have a queen. Instead, the Duchess of Cornwall. A bit of a giggle for residents of a town in Ontario. But others may associate Camilla's sobriquet with Robert Browning's bleak poem — "My Last Duchess."

"I gave commands / Then all smiles stopped together ..."

But the duchess who will likely visit Canada in company with King Charles the ? should fare better. We've rarely had a real duchess to drop the ceremonial puck at Maple Leaf Gardens, and the game can use a bit of class, after Todd Bertuzzi.

And one would hope that, meantime, Prince Charles fares better on a visit to Canada than did his grand-uncle, Prince Edward, whose most memorable moment was falling off a horse in Alberta. It was all downhill for Ed after that equine descent, as he also fell for Mrs. Wallis Simpson (an American, of all people!) and abandoned the throne before he fell off it.

More recently, on his honeymoon visit to Scotland, Prince Charles wore a kilt. This showed off the royal knees and should have intimidated the Loch Ness Monster. So what does Charles wear to visit Canada? We are reminded that we have no national dress other than the maple leaf, which provides less coverage than the kilt.

These potential problems for Charles the Whatever encourage Canadians to really mean it when we sing "God Save the Queen." Not that we wish him ill fortune. It's just that a King Harold or a King William would be easier to number, as a first. Especially since we colonials have trouble recognizing any number lower than 99.

CHOOSING YOUR DOCTOR

Your choice of doctor can affect your health. Forget about your other relationships, such as spouse, tax accountant, broker — as relatively minor factors in your well-being. Focus on your physician. The critical criteria:

*Qualifications. Okay, so this doctor has been recommended by a family member who may or may not benefit from your demise. What else do you know about this doctor? Any initials *after* his or her name? (M.D. is good, but watch for D.V.M. [veterinarian], R.M.T. [massage], P.D.Q., etc.)

Are older doctors more reliable than younger doctors? Not necessarily. An older doctor will have seen it all, or at least glimpsed most of it, so that your condition should come as no surprise, or have mostly novelty value. But the older doctor probably has his own health problems, and may regard yours with ill-concealed contempt if you have taken sick leave from *your* job, while he is stiff-upper-lipping to attend to your whining.

*The doctor's nurse/secretary.** If there is a prematurely aged woman sitting in the foyer of the doctor's office, openly sobbing, or just staring at the telephone as though it were a coiled cobra, you know that the doctor has more patients than he can deal with effectively, plus those too weak to dial. This is the clearest warning sign after his office's revolving door.

On the other hand, if the doctor's nurse greets you with a charming smile and says throatily, "The doctor will be with you shortly," you know that his nurse is on drugs. Since the doctor is likely aware that his overworked and chronically stoned nurse stays on the job only because he is a cheap and reliable source of coke or meth, you should hesitate to roll up your sleeve, let alone drop your pants.

*The doctor's waiting room.** The clearest evidence that your doctor cares about your survival.

Not a phone booth with pretensions. Because, let's face it, you will be spending most of your doctor-visit time in his or her waiting room. Patients who are *very* sick may well spend what remains of their lives in that oubliette. Rigor-mortised for their appointment with purgatory.

This is why — before you commit your one and only body to his care — it is essential that you conduct a thorough examination, with a clipboard, of your potential doctor's waiting room. Here are some of the crucial requirements to be met:

1. Ample square footage. You do not want to have to sit beside a person who is sick or he wouldn't be there. And who is

hacking and sneezing without putting a bag over his head. A germ geyser. Radiating a miasma that could put paid to your life expectancy.

2. Ideally, your doctor's waiting room has *chairs*. (If it's standing room only, it means that the doctor is expecting a percentage of patients to die before he can see them.) Are the chairs lining the walls (less chance of your inhaling a bug you didn't come in with), or ranged in row after row

(indicating a house capacity rivalling that of the Met)?

Now, it may not be realistic to look for a doctor whose waiting-room space rivals that of an airplane hangar. Unless he is a country doctor working out of a horse and buggy, his office rent is reflected in how he gives you a rectal — i.e., brutal.

3. Music. Every doctor recognizes the value of taped music in a waiting room as a factor in making the patient sedated before the diagnosis of a suspect lump. Marching tunes are surgically removed. As are love songs. (At least 25 percent of male patients are there because of incipient sexual impotence. The last thing they want to sit there hearing is Perry Como singing "Can't Get Enough of You.")

Finally, try to find out whether your tentative doctor makes house calls. Or even flat calls. It's a rare service. Instead, the person abed with a minor bug is referred to 911. And the emergency summons means the arrival on your street of three ambulances, sirens wailing, drawing a crowd of neighbours curious to know the cause of your desperate condition, in case it's pandemic.

Less sensational is just to learn to live with your labial lumbago (stiff upper lip). Plus the medical support of a mature Medoc.

CLUELESS IN GAZA

For years, growing up in the form of a teenager living in a somewhat demure community, I thought that an erection was a Japanese election. Our sex education depended on what we picked up in the gutter. My neighbourhood was too poor to have a gutter. I had a ditch — a poor source of sexual enlightenment.

I never really bought the belief that babies are delivered by stork. We had no storks in our part of British Columbia, but a lot of babies. Besides, storks could be shot down by guys whose plans had not included fatherhood.

My parents displayed on the mantelpiece a baby photo of me holding a rubber ball over the genital area. This undoubtedly influenced my writing … later. And may explain why I was never very good at playing cricket.

Under the influence of positive thinking, I tried to handle pain by keeping a stiff upper lip. This resulted in labial paralysis. A fixed grin inappropriate for a professional humorist. I now find that I get more relief from pain by whining a lot. The pain is miraculously transferred to the asses of relatives. It is a Lourdes without the cost of pilgrimage.

Watching the birds and the bees was equally futile, while getting my face stung by a bee that seemed to resent my research.

I don't remember my first kiss, but I suspect that it was the girl who took the initiative. She regretted it immediately, as I was quickly all over her, a torrent of passion. Her name, I don't remember, but I am sure that the recipient was a girl. Although I didn't know at the time that I was heterosexual. The term had not yet come into common parlance. So, instead my fear was that I was otherwise abnormal — a closet sex fiend.

I suspected that my susceptibility to sexual arousal made me a pervert. Having to wear a trench coat to the high school dance made that social activity impractical. So, I concentrated on becoming introverted. *La vie intérieure* I lived to the full. My sexual fantasies were not Disney material, but they did provide something to go to bed with.

Now middle-aged, my kids don't appear to hold a grudge about the circumstances of their conception. They may even assume that I was happy to see them, again and again, in a hospital neonatal ward. But feelings don't get more mixed than those I had, having to lean on my pencil to support a growing crowd.

Are today's young people better off, mentally if not physically, for their greater freedom from sexual restraint? They certainly appear to be. Which I find annoying. To have it all without gagging on some of it makes them less prepared to handle the slap in the face that Fate will deal them. And somehow I will get the medical bill.

Well, these periods of moral decline are cyclical. The Roman age was followed by the Crusades. The racy Restoration by Queen Victoria, looking down her nose for distances as far as the colonies. What it will take to pull up our moral socks, I can't guess. With any luck it will come after, if not as a result of, my passing from the libidinous scene.

Meantime, regarding the current dress style of girls, I suspect that skirts are up to no good. Otherwise I applaud the ascent and look forward to the sitting down. Simple pleasures, but why look for complexity? Ah, sweet mystery of life, where did you go?

COMBAT ZONE

Men Shopping Suffer Same Mental Stress as in War Battles
— News Item

Scene: A Starbucks in the battlefield of a megamall. Two haggard male shoppers — Bill and Mike — slump on stools. Mike is bleeding from a facial wound inflicted by a parkade pillar. Their white-knuckle hands, clutching mugs of coffee, still tremble from the horror their bloodshot eyes have witnessed. And their twitching cheeks show the strain of five hours' Christmas shopping without access to a privy.

BILL: Which sector you been in, mate?

MIKE: Ladies underwear. [He is still traumatized by the horror.]

BILL: The aisles of hell. You're going to need counselling, mate.

MIKE: I know. I … I just about bought it. [He shudders.] Got caught in a crossfire of thongs.

BILL: Deadly. Me, I tried to take out a negligee.

MIKE: For yourself?

BILL: For my wife! I swear I wouldn't be in lingerie for anyone else!

MIKE: I believe you, mate. I had the same trouble in that sector, establishing myself as heterosexual. I learned to show the clerk this. [He produces a card on which is printed: I AM A GUY BUYING THIS FOR HIS WIFE. PLEASE DO NOT SHOW ME YOUR NAUGHTY KNICKERS.]

BILL: Has that helped?

MIKE: Not a bit.

BILL: It figures. I'm guessing you're heterosexual … right?

MIKE: I was when I came into this place. Now I'm not sure …

BILL: I know the feeling. Shelf-shock. How long you been in this sector?

MIKE: I don't know. I've lost track of time. I can't even remember where I parked my car.

BILL: Is it a recent model?

MIKE: It was before I came in here. [He takes a grubby envelope from his pocket.] I got a letter from home, while I was pinned down in hardware. From my wife. She says she's leaving me. And suing me for desertion. [Tearful, Mike blows his nose on his sleeve, noisily enough to wake up several clerks.] That means I have to return the tool set I just bought her.

Eric Nicol

CONFESSION OF AN AGNOSTIC

Having an open mind can create a draft in your beliefs.

Mine has been ajar for so many years now I have difficulty believing in whatever. A sorry state of affairs, especially sexual affairs.

This incredulity dates from my being a youthful university student, full of piss and Voltaire. I rejected religious belief as a crutch for the gimpy mind. I developed a strong faith in skepticism. And raised an eyebrow at any assertion not based on demonstrable fact, priding myself on my absence of belief in anything abstract. I became convinced that if Charles Darwin had not come up with the theory of evolution, I would have twigged to it on the basis of observing the simian behaviour of fraternity members.

I attributed my aversion to orthodox religion to a sturdy skepticism, a readiness to doubt almost anything not grounded on fact. My best friend was Sam Stone with whom I shared a religious devotion to Ping-Pong.

I felt embarrassed having to sing "God Save the King," hearing it as invoking salvation of the archaic by the inconceivable.

When obliged to join one of Canada's armed services in the Second World War, on the tenuous assumption that I might help to achieve the Allies' victory over Nazi Germany and fascist Italy, I flummoxed the recruiting officer inscribing my dossier when he asked, "Religion?"

"No, thanks," I said. He was not amused, so I added, "I'm an agnostic, sir."

It was immediately apparent that he had not heard of this credo, conditioned as he was to tick off either Catholic or Anglican, occasionally Sikh.

"Agnostic?" he queried, impatient to slot my soul and get on to my body. "What's that?"

"Agnostic, sir, means that I don't subscribe to any orthodox religion."

"You're an *atheist*?" I could tell that the word offended him. "You don't believe in *God*?"

"I have an open mind about a supreme being. I just don't pray as much as when I had eczema." I was hoping that mention of the medical condition might excuse me from overactive service, but the recruiting officer was not to be diverted from my consecration.

"I'm putting you down as Protestant," he said.

"Protestant will be fine, sir. I protest regularly."

Today I can smile at the excessive rationalism of my youth. If I had got killed in action — and I contend that I was not — the air force would not have known whether to bury me in Latin or just with sober mumbling.

But I can understand why there are no atheists in the trenches. The decline in trench warfare has been bad for organized religion.

And I, too, have mellowed a bit, permitting myself a small smile at the current tizzy between the evolutionists and the intelligent-design disciples. And I'm sticking with the Darwinians. Even though my hair is thinning, the physical resemblance to the simian is unmistakable. Thus endeth the controversy.

Yet billions of other people on this pleasantly atypical planet continue to believe that their progenitor was divinely created, popped into the Garden of Eden clean-shaven and ready to accept the apple being flogged by Eve, wearing a provocative fig leaf.

We also know that life on this amiable globe is doomed to a violent demise, guaranteed to ruin our day. So why — knowing all this — am I flossing my teeth with that passionate devotion once reserved for the flagellants? Do I think that St. Peter might be a sucker for a nice smile?

Okay, I'll buy that — if it's on special.

Eric Nicol

DANCE FLOORED

I did not attend my high school graduation party. Reason: I had heard on good authority that this event included dancing. An activity that I knew would involve me in a close encounter with that mysterious object: a girl.

Just *thinking* about grasping one of those creatures around the waist caused a disturbance in my pants that could not be blamed on bad tailoring. No, it had to be erectile dementia. A condition I blamed on my Scots ancestry. The reason for their wearing a kilt. Whereas the English can be comfortable in trousers.

I lived with this handicap until the outbreak of the Second World War made me realize I might die a virgin unless I could control the lust that lurked below the belt. So I signed up for dance lessons. Being able to waltz, I reckoned, would condition me for a degree of contact with a girl without the nether obtrusion. It would be money well spent, if it kept me out of jail on an assault charge.

My major oversight in this plan: my dance instructor was *a woman.* Worse, a very attractive woman. Who on meeting showed no apprehension at having to deal with a budding sex maniac.

"What steps would you like to learn?" she asked me.

"Uh, the waltz?" I had watched enough Hollywood musicals to know that the waltz was performed at arm's length. The tango would have to come later, if at all.

"First, take my hand." As she had offered that appendage, I had little choice. "Now put your other arm around my waist."

Even though this phase came as no surprise, I all too obviously wasn't ready for it. My cheek tingled, in anticipation of getting slapped. My mind was yelling, "Abort! Abort!"

But I did put my arm around her waist. And immediately regretted it.

"Ow!" I cried, backing off.

"What's wrong?"

"My back just went out," I whined.

My back was not what had gone out, but the truth could have got me arrested for indecent assault. I hastily handed my instructor enough twenties to teach me a lesson with no redeeming features.

Thereafter I regarded myself as a sex pervert. And I tried to look at any woman as if she were my mother. On a bad day, my grandmother.

I avoided looking at suggestive food such as peaches and bananas, thus consuming a lot of fruit worms.

Today, as an old guy, I can look back wistfully at those days of involuntary movement. I am still not waltzing. My front has quieted down, but my back goes out. Belatedly, my wife assures me that an erection is the most sincere compliment that a man can pay a woman. There was really no need for me to wear a raincoat on so many dates. There was no precipitation.

I have to conclude that for men there is no stage of life when we are completely at ease with our genitals. They are *appendages*. Our body has never fully accepted them as other than undependable adjutants hanging out to make trouble.

Don't risk the rhumba,

DEAR DIRT

Dirt cheap. A phrase that is overdue for retirement. Because, of course, *dirt is no longer cheap*. It has changed its name to *soil*. Fertilizer is soil food. And the jewel of my garden is the compost heap. Because that is where my precious soil is generated. I like to stand beside it and listen to the worms crapping to make me more dirt.

Dirty nails? Think of them as wealth at your fingertips! All hail humus!

Today dirt is delivered in an armoured car. I haven't ordered any for years, opting to pay a kid's university fees.

Dirt is now so valued that it is no longer environmentally chic to be buried in a casket. We have to remember what happened with the pharaohs of ancient Egypt. Not content with a quiet family cremation, they had themselves *entombed* in pyramids. Result: the Sahara Desert. Have we learned *nothing* from King Tut?

My apologies. I didn't intend to become emotional about dirt. I'm a bit touchy since my neighbour built a fence that cut off my dirt heap from sunlight. Irradiated dirt is recognized to be the best milieu for growing plants bigger than your neighbour's. Like, sunflowers. I have a dirt-fed sunflower that burps seeds big enough to stun small insects. Mother Nature in your face, neighbour!

Sadly, proper respect for dirt is a guy thing. Women have a gene that makes them hate dirt, attack it on sight. I belong to the cadre of guys who believe the vacuum cleaner had to be invented by a woman. Hilda Hoover. Who had had an unfortunate love affair with a dirt farmer who never wiped his boots, or even took them off.

That's why women need to be educated regarding the global value of dirt. Also we need more male teachers in elementary school, where at present the preponderance of female teachers brainwashes boys, who grow up with terraphobia, or chronic guilt about their belly button lint.

More positive would be teaching that the main reason why Canada is the most peace-loving state on Earth is that Canada has an abundance of dirt. The Middle East has shown how touchy people can become when they are short of dirt. The desert makes even the camel short-tempered.

DEILOGUE

Setting: An upscale bistro near Purgatory. God and Satan have sat down together over a beer. The Devil is buying. The Lord is the less relaxed.

"So, Jehovah," says Satan, "how's it going with that whatsit you created — mankind?"

God snorts, expanding several universes.

"Those twits! Would you believe it? A lot of them are still taking my name in vain!"

"No shit. Slow learners, eh?"

"Some don't even believe in me anymore, let alone what's in the Book."

The Devil nods, wryly. "Tell me about it."

"They don't believe in you, either?"

"I couldn't get arrested. In Toronto, even."

"You mean Satan's palace isn't hacking it as a forwarding address?"

"Uh-uh. The whole Inferno's cooling down, relatively. Competition from global warming. The hotter the Earth gets, the less people fear going to hell."

"Bummer."

"Also our River Styx has got polluted. Souls of damned agnostics! Who knew?"

"I did. But then I know everything, whether I want to or not." The Lord sighs, blowing away some of Japan's smaller islands. "Just between you and me, Heaven, too, isn't like the old days when you were an angel. I hate to admit it, Meph, but you did liven up the place for a while."

The Devil nods. "We had some spirited debates up there. Now …" Tears well in Satan's eyes and promptly turn to steam. "Hell is a forking bore."

"Infernal nuisance, eh?" The Almighty takes a drag on his stogie, creating panic in parts of Mongolia. "But at least you're drawing larger crowds down there."

"SRO. But they're mostly tinhorn sinners. We're not getting the big fish — the Hitlers, the Casanovas — the major-league bunch of damned souls. That Emperor Caligula — there was a sweetie." Satan shakes his head wistfully. "No offence, Lord, but they don't seem to build creeps like that anymore."

The Almighty frowns into his lager. "Purgatory," he mutters.

"Pardon me?"

"I've got a surfeit of souls parked in Purgatory these days. Who would have thought divine justice would bog down in litigation?"

"Too many damn lawyers! One of my few pleasures these days is popping a shyster on the barbie."

The two primordial rivals watch glumly as the soul of a determinist drifts past their table, thumbing his nose at them.

God muses, "I can't remember why I kicked you out of Heaven."

"Because I wanted your job."

"Ah, so you did." God's splendid eyes narrow. "Do you still want it?"

"Change places with you? Are you kidding? Hades is no hell."

"Mmm. No nuns." The Almighty chews morosely on his manna, then says, "It seemed like a promising idea at the time."

"What did?"

"Evolution. On Earth. Just pepper a planet with a bunch of chemicals to create life in a few billion years, then wait to see what happens."

"No joy?"

"Dinosaurs, for my sake! Great bloody monsters tearing up everything that moved! The dinosaurs laid an egg!"

"That why you had to scrub them?"

"Of course. And I replaced them with an even bigger pain in the astral complex."

"Homo sap."

"Which makes the dinosaurs look like choirboys." The Lord shakes his head ruefully, putting a topspin on Mars. "Human beans!"

"I believe it's human *beings*, God."

"Whatever. Did you ever get a good look at one of those freaks, naked, in the flabby flesh?"

"Emetic — right?"

"Ugliest damn ape ever to swing out of a tree. Then pee on Creation!"

"And what about that Adam and Eve thing!" Satan snorts. "Casting me as a snake pushing apples! Talk about low-grade temptation!"

"And now that overblown chimp is claiming I don't exist at all! Prattling about 'the Big Bang' as creator of their expanding universe! Crediting my lovely firmament to 'dark matter.' Do I look like a darkie to you?"

"Around Hades the scoop is that you once had it off with a flying horse."

"No, that was Zeus. Roman god. Gave the whole pantheon a bad name. I've had to clean up his act. But do I get respect?"

They order another beer. God springs for it.

"So," asks Satan, "what's your next gig?"

God, like Atlas, shrugs. "I'm seriously thinking of retiring."

"*Retiring?*" The Devil — who thought he had heard everything — was so shocked one of his horns fell off. "You're retiring from *creating*?"

"I'm afraid it's become compulsive. Flawing my omniscience. I should have known that human beings make poor souls."

"You can't have them re-souled, so to speak?"

God shakes his head, rattling the Pearly Gates. "They've had their chance. I even made it easier to get to Heaven by replacing the stairway with an escalator."

"Tech doesn't get any higher."

"Then one old soul trips on the escalator and tries to sue me for damages to her halo. Lucky thing, all the lawyers have gone down to your place."

"Hell has a speed elevator."

"The bottom line is, from now on I'm granting immortal souls on the basis of merit. Starting with dogs."

"Really? I thought dogs already had them. The way they look at a person …"

"Yes, my admissions committee has been judging by the wrong end. The tail was not conclusive."

"So, bye-bye Saint Peter, hello, St. Bernard."

"Right. And I have another project you might find amusing."

"What's that?"

"To renovate Hell as the ultimate in underground parks."

"Tell me more, Big Daddy!"

"The damned soul is doomed to go around and around for eternity, looking for a space to park."

"And all the levels have the same letter — *H*!"

"And the concrete pillars shift when you try to back in!"

"And you never see another living soul to help you find the way out!"

"The sign EXIT means nothing!"

"Blank wall! RESERVED FOREVER. I love it!" The Devil raises his glass to toast the Lord. "Thanks a bunch, Almighty!"

"My pleasure. The next round's on you."

DOGGEREL

Okay, so you've tried having a wife or husband, and now you're ready to settle for having a dog. Wrong attitude! A dog should never be regarded as a substitute for a spouse. Unless, of course, the spouse stood on all fours. In which case you should be dating a shrink.

Next decision: small dog or big dog? Dachshund or Great Dane? Small dogs are more demonstrative than large dogs, and if your small dog craps on the floor, your house doesn't need to be demolished. But a large dog is better positioned to lick your face, if you have no other source of adulation.

Although small dogs are yappy, and large dogs crappy, all dogs are naturally happy to be alive and sniffing turd. They may not purr, like a cat, but the other end is more expressive, and likely to convey delight.

If your dog food bill is apt to be a factor in your being able to afford to feed yourself, the Pekinese is a prudent choice. However, your Peke will be more yappy, and the Airedale more crappy, compared to a dogfish.

You also may want a dog that doesn't "shed," i.e., it has no coat. This restricts your choice to naturally naked dogs. However, naturally naked dogs tend to be more touchy than shaggy dogs, whose vision is naturally obscured from seeing things to get hysterical about.

Some women buy a big dog to protect them from uninvited advances by men. They are outnumbered by the women walking small dogs. Or no dog at all.

As a kid, I lived with a terrier named Spot (for the obvious reason). Spot chased a tennis ball when I hit the ball against our garage door. This provided me, as an only child, with company of a sort, except that Spot made a game of not returning the ball to me. He would tease me with the prospect, so I had to feign indifference about ever seeing the ball again. Study my fingernails, and yawn, till he coughed up.

This meant my going through a hell of a lot of tennis balls without ever seeing a court. Then I concluded that Spot thought I was hitting the tennis balls because I was mad at them. (Sometimes I *was* mad at them, blaming them for a flawed backhand, forehand, and service. But I wasn't seeking a permanent divorce.)

Because Spot had a troubled relationship with our postman, I was able to blame him for not getting replies from publishers. I would have had a fatter acceptance file with a cat. (A rationale, perhaps, but it seems to have worked for Cardinal Richelieu.)

Also, a cat doesn't need to be walked. It walks itself. Sometimes too far to ever be seen again. But no pet is perfect. And the unfortunate fact is that a cat's affection is heavily dependent on its being fed. On time. There's no deadline for a dog's loyalty. Whereas a cat's begins to wane roughly five seconds after it's fed.

A dog will not only forgive you your trespasses, it will trespass in places you find hard to reach. Just don't acquire a large breed. Unless your plans include sleeping in a tent together.

Note: the best name for a dog is Alf. Which sounds barky enough to get the dog's attention …

DRESSED TO SELL

One reason — maybe the only reason — why I'm not widely recognized as a writer is that I'm not dressed for it. I don't own a smoking jacket.

(I'm afraid it would aggravate my hay fever.) In fact, I don't smoke at all unless really, really annoyed.

But I do recognize the importance, for a writer, of owning a tweedy jacket with patched elbows. To date my elbows haven't been sharp enough — despite being spoken to — for the jacket to establish me as a literary figure.

A pity, this. I'm convinced I would be invited to appear on more TV talk shows if my clothes had aged gracefully. But I shouldn't blame my elbows. They're still supporting most of my weight when I'm praying for relief from spam and other computer problems.

Some authors are foolish enough to do a TV interview wearing *a suit*, for Pete's sake. Intact elbows, a zipped fly, *creased trousers*! What madness! They're trying to look as though a copy of their book has actually been sold. To someone outside their family. In a proper bookstore. "Tsk!" And I repeat, "tsk!"

Posthumously, yes. When feeling mortal, I may dress for lying in state, if state is having a slow day. I think mourners will respect my wearing my clean runners, the matched pair with laces. (I never wear leather shoes anymore. Poor traction. Deadly on hills. Writers who die with their boots on have been asking for trouble.)

I haven't worn a necktie for fifty years, being convinced that even occasional necktie wearing can make a man impotent. Instead, my vestment of choice is the turtleneck shirt. My own neck having aged into a reptilian aspect, a turtleneck shirt may be deemed a tad redundant. But it's a boon to arthritic fingers, for whom knotting a cravat could become a life work.

Thus I have this lifetime supply of neckties I never wear. I guess they would have sentimental value if I could remember who gave them to me.

As for shoe wear, I'm dedicated to runners, even though I now don't run in any situation other than escape from a tidal wave. I still believe it's possible to achieve fame without having to wear shoes.

But the fact is, loafers are for bakery workers and writers. Both crafts subject to public appearance.

A closet writer dies with his boots off.

Meanwhile, in the same way that Groucho Marx used his cigar as a prop for his monologues, the novice writer should adopt some signature device for recognition by people who don't read but buy books as gifts for friends or relatives.

There is no point in an author hanging around the bookstore, hoping to be recognized if he or she is dressed like an ordinary mortal.

Note: regardless of what the author wears, there is no guarantee that a bookstore's autographing session won't prove to be three hours of hellish isolation, punctuated only by visits from the store manager to ensure that the author hasn't become mortified remains. Keep tapping that loafered toe!

EERIE MAIL

Checking our email. The morning ritual second only to checking our fly. Or mumbling our morning prayer. God may forgive us our trespasses, but not our ignoring the message from *jehovah.com*

Our email can have priority over a bowel movement. The content may be as fecal, but the process is rarely as cathartic.

At any given moment, millions of people sit staring at their computer, waiting for that little black arrowhead — the curser, I call it — to confirm that the menu is all spam.

Before our mail became electronic, we could judge something of the sender's character from the cut of his or her script. A curvy consonant, the rakishly crossed *t*, the forward slant of all letters —

these spoke volumes about the character of the sender. Women still become aroused just looking at Casanova's letters to a target duchess.

In earlier times, we could see that a love letter had been mimeographed. Or even Xeroxed. But email casts serious doubt on the singularity of the receiver. The *billet doux* one receives may be a mass mailing second only to Sears.

And email has no scent. Personal letters used to bear the fragrance that identified the sender in case the name had slipped our memory. Email is mute *and* scentless. It is best suited to informing relatives that a family member has died.

Emailing can easily become so addictive that it thins time available for more productive or meaningful activities. Like work. Its attachments alone may impair other, more meaningful engagements, such as marriage, or even personal hygiene.

My doubts about intercourse dependent on telephone poles are aggravated by there being no definitive spelling for the wretched thing. Is it *email*, or *e-mail*? Any word that can't make up its mind about being hyphenated — dictionaries accept both, to their everlasting shame — deserves scorn.

I have more respect for Indian smoke signals.

However, the most sinister feature of email is that *it can be almost impossible to get rid of*. Appealing to the "delete" button is of no avail. The computer merely hides the email in the rotting matter of deleted items. Waiting for the chance to reappear and haunt the recipient like Marley's ghost.

Thus the only way to exorcize one's email, with its evidence that fully justifies the litigant's petition for divorce plus damages, is to kill one's computer. And bury it at sea. Therefore email *must* be answered. The protocol is inexorable. A person may be derelict in other behaviour — forget to zip his fly, fail to floss after brushing — without arousing suspicion that the old mentis is now compost — but his email is imperious.

Finally, one should be leery of any messaging that depends heavily on electricity. Despite the prevalence of wall plugs, nobody fully understands electricity. No juice, no use. This is why email will never replace our postman. Who is often the nicest part of communicative intercourse. Right?

EGGING ON SPERM

A team of single-minded scientists has found that the mammalian egg ("ma" for short) emits a chemical message *that beckons male sperm*. And there is not a darn thing Canadian broadcasting authorities can do about it.

For years men have naively believed that their sperm was protected enough by a jockstrap. Not, obviously, so. That dogged egg lurking in the reproductive system of the lady sitting beside you on the bus is silently transmitting, via her ovaries, a signal to your unsuspecting sperm. Crossing your knees won't help. It is *sub rosa* seduction. Yet you are the one more likely to be arrested and charged with molestation.

This jeopardy is aggravated by the fact that it is increasingly difficult to tell, at a glance, whether a woman has stopped laying eggs. What appears to be an old crone may be still harbouring a randy ovum, whereas a young wench could have blown all her eggs on one bastard.

Now that scientists have found that bawdy eggs are making passes at guys' sperm, what can the victims do to protect themselves from this invisible sexual assault? Wearing lead-lined undershorts seems impractical, slowing down progress in a variety of activities.

Even more problematic is a guy trying to establish a timetable for when a female companion is ovulating. And it is almost impossible to determine whether his date is laying an egg, womb-wise. Most of us never give the matter a single thought, blinded as we are by those parts of a woman closer to the surface.

What we *can* watch is this continuing research into cell biology, in particular the makeup of the chemical homing signal that entices the sperm to get involved with the egg. Meanwhile, the boffins say that *their* job is to find a solution for some forms of infertility. Apparently, there are some people — probably of the unfair sex — who consider infertility to be a drawback to becoming parents. They fail to see that infertility is Mother Nature's way of saying "Enough, already!"

Clearly, for scientists the first priority should be to establish: how close does the woman's egg need to be to the guy's sperm for the egg's chemical message to put the hit on him? Ten feet? A city block? A country mile? Never underestimate the carrying power of a lure from the egg of a woman set on parturition.

Another question: how much depends, in terms of a guy maintaining a blithesome lifestyle free of diaper changing, on how receptive his sperm is? Especially in perilous conditions such as church picnics and office parties where liquor is apt to lurk. Sperm that has had a few too many glasses of plonk may let its guard down. Even though the guy came mostly for the chocolate cake.

Anyhow, at least men now know — or should know once word gets around the golf course — that Mother Nature isn't called that just because she looks homey in an apron. Under it lurks the chemically loaded, semen-hunting egg. The *oeuf* with oomph.

And a guy's sperm, which he fondly believed to be out of harm's way if he said his prayers — sheesh, pawn fertilizer!

EXIT SIGNS

Demise-wise, I am hoping to die in my sleep. From a heart attack induced by an erotic dream. This aspiration is not yet fulfilled, owing to my waking up in the morning. My subconscious is goofing off to join other mental delinquents.

"Who," to paraphrase Hamlet in one of his many distraught moments, "would not his own quietus make with a bare bodkin?" So far as I remember, I don't have a bodkin, in the kitchen drawer, bare or fully clothed.

Meanwhile I waste a lot of my waking time scratching my head as part of the creative writing process. Maybe I should be scratching elsewhere. In any event, my head scratching has yet to produce a best-selling novel. Instead I have a remarkably healthy head of hair. Mocking bald writers who haven't put enough ponderation into their work.

"Heaven gives its favourites an early death," sayeth the poet, probably after a bad day at the Orphean. If the race form is accurate, I am obviously not a favourite. I have blown my innocence. Being naive — something I am still very good at — doesn't earn any brownie points with paradise.

Given another career choice, I would certainly go for astronomer. It's not just that the astronomer gets to sit down a lot. The lure of a disability pension warranted by my permanent crick in the neck from ogling an asteroid? Irresistible.

However, that is just *my* problem. Possibly a larger question is whether we are depending too heavily on reasoning to interpret the mysteries of the universe. Overly preoccupied with trying to find the meaning of natural phenomena. This conclusion is one hard for astral scientists to accept, if they're getting government funding.

It is easier for me, as a fully documented layman, to concentrate on the meaning of my own life as it stumbles off the stage. Everything considered, I would have to say that the major regret of my life is that I never learned to dance the tango. I guess I just wasn't Latin enough. Genetically disadvantaged.

Also I would have to say that I have been too sexually inhibited to wear tight pants. Except at the waist. Which doesn't count as aphrodisiac.

On the plus side, my bedroom mirror has never been a major object of preoccupation. In fact, I am always a bit surprised to see myself in it. The reflection appears to be shocked to see me, too. We both get the hell out of there before it becomes traumatizing.

To improve my chances of dying in my sleep, I retire with a pillow over my head. Allegedly to muffle the dawn chirps of oversexed robins, but practically to encourage a nice, quiet suffocation.

"Those whom the gods love, die young." Well, I guess I didn't catch their fancy. Bunch of queers, likely. Wearing those gowns, what would you expect?

My final dictum on dress: clothes make the man, but it's what's under them that makes the woman. The rest is window shopping. So, don't be a dummy. Don't stand in the window.

GUILT COMPLEXITY

As a senior and long-time motorist, I feel partly responsible for global warming. It doesn't top my sin list, but it is the easiest to discuss in public. And live with without having to change something personal.

So when it recently came time to buy a new car, I went to a dealership selling small Japanese models that my research had identified as merely sipping gas, with moderate emissions, and a deferential attitude toward the environment. The salesman introduced me to a diminutive red sedan. The price exceeded my budget, but I was seduced by the rear-window washer, a luxury-defying restraint.

I bought the little red car. And we lived happily together ... for several hours. Then, having reason to move backward, I discovered that the car was disinclined to reverse. There was an *R* on the gearshift, but the car refused to acknowledge it.

A request to proceed in any direction but forward — an admirable attitude, but not compatible with parking in my garage, which is not a drive-through.

So I returned the car to the dealership, whose staff looked incredulous when I recounted the glitch in the brief relationship. They held a hurried meeting backstage, while I waited in their very comfortable guest room, and I saw them glancing at my grey hair, worriedly, as though fearful that my senility might become excretory.

Ultimately, they dispatched a mechanic to confirm that the car had no problem backing, and this customer was a fruitcake heavy on the nuts. The mechanic returned looking haggard. Another hurried conference to which I was not invited, though I thought I heard sobbing. I braced myself for a hara-kiri ceremony. Then a well-dressed, senior-executive type emerged to say to me, "We shall need to repair. Please to wait in lounge."

After lounging for another three hours, mulling the old adage, "Once a dud, always a dud," I was reunited with my little red sedan. And, praise the Lord, it *backed*. I backed it again and again, for the sheer joy of reversing, whooping and alarming an elderly lady who may have been contemplating a purchase.

Driving home blithely, I noticed a reaction from other drivers somehow motivated to show me their middle finger. Something about my red car brought out the bull in them as they aimed their horns at my backside. I quickly learned: when driving a red car, if you *must* change lanes, activate the turn signal the previous day. While extending your left arm out the window brandishing a sign: YOO-HOO! AM INITIATING A LANE CHANGE! PRAY FOR ME!

Another lesson I was to learn: police hand out tickets to a red car *even when it is parked.* Yes, in a legal zone. The charge: failure to wear a seat belt. I was necking with a girl in the front seat at the time. To have tried to do so while strapped in could have caused serious body damage not covered by insurance.

The bottom line: the safest colour for your car is that of the cop's — black. Dark black. Or dark white. You may confirm this by dialing 911 and saying, "Police, please," though this is harder to say than it looks.

But if you insist on keeping your red car, as I did mine, you should not only pause at a stop sign but back up a little. Some other drivers, in non-red vehicles, are easily provoked if they are already having a bad day.

Note: equipping your red car with a siren, while not unlawful, may tempt you to use it. With consequences too ugly to contemplate.

GUN SHY

Mea bloody culpa. I owe the other gun-loving guys of Canada an apology. For probably being the main reason why the government felt obliged to enact the gun-registry law. Ottawa finally realized that I was a gun freak, and it took the measures necessary to keep tabs on my old .22.

My intimate relationship with firearms began when I was a kid, reading nothing but westerns (Zane Grey) and attending the Saturday matinee horse opera at the local cinema. Where bullets flew with gay abandon.

True, I identified with the good guy (white hat), but from age six to sixteen my life was trigger-happy. I never met a gun I couldn't like.

The first I owned (at eight) was a homemade weapon: a clothes peg nailed to a butt of broom handle, discharging a rubber band with enough force to nail the bad guy (usually a fly on the wall).

Tired of cleaning walls, as a fourteenth birthday present, my parents gave me a .22 rifle. Which I used to shoot rats under our back porch. A pastime that may have been a factor in the rapid turnover of neighbours in our block.

With the onset of the Second World War, and the threat of assault on Vancouver by the Japanese navy, and with no defence except the old Nine O'clock Gun in Stanley Park, I readied my .22 for a last stand as an alternative to running like hell.

But when the Americans dropped the atomic bomb on Hiroshima, my .22 rifle became less vital to the defence of the free world. And the collapse of the Axis turned attention to our privately owned weapons of mass destruction. I was ready to use mine to deal with the menace that replaced Hitler: the skunk that came into our backyard every night for the express purpose of dropping a nuclear stench that I would not have chosen as part of our home-security system.

I loaded my old .22. My wife made me unload it. She didn't trust my aim or ability to distinguish a skunk from our next-door neighbour wearing a striped nightshirt. Then, to make doubly sure that the skunk was home free, Canada's government instituted the gun registry. I tried to explain to Ottawa that my wife had made me impotent, weapons-wise, but they didn't answer my letter.

As the final ignominy, I had to have my photo taken to accompany my gun registration form. This passport-style photo captures my anti-social, possibly sex pervert image. Just having the thing in the house has impaired my confidence in handling the old .22. Ballistically, I'm impotent.

If I were an American, this would never happen. U.S. citizens buy and sell guns with a blithe spirit I can only envy. Shoot!

HABERDASHERY FOR HUMORISTS

I have been identified as a humorist. This has placed severe restrictions on what I can wear — in public at least — without damaging my image as a person not to be taken seriously, if at all. If clothes make the man, I'm unmade.

Hoping to come across as insouciant, I haven't bought a new suit for twenty years. I wear pants that would be rejected by the Salvation Army. The legs cross without me in them. The pants do have a zipper, but it is an elderly model that can become absent-minded in social situations.

Thanks to arthritic fingers and back, tying my shoelaces is a project that requires careful planning. A faulty loop can bring traffic to a crashing halt. Thus I must exercise special vigilance when dressing for social occasions that require putting on shoes that I'm not familiar with. My son recently got married, despite my generous offer if they would just elope. During the ceremony, I gazed fixedly at my feet. Other guests may have thought I was lost in praying for the union. Actually, the knot tying that worried me was below my ankle.

Naturally, I avoid new shoes. The laces aren't broken in. Feisty, they can be. So I wear runners that have thousands of miles on them. Without ever being run. (Just one of several body movements that are history.) The tread is still good on my runners, but I suspect they may be running on their own. I can't watch them *all* the time.

While on the subject of my relationship with my footwear, I'll confess that I don't change my socks as often as would be compatible with Earth's atmosphere. I certainly don't tussle with them just to go to bed. What an inane exercise that would be! Unless your bare feet have some kind of illicit relationship going on, making your back pay for hauling off your socks — ridiculous!

When your socks start walking without you, sure, it may be time for a change. And as for leaving them on when you're taking a shower. Just to save time for more important matters than personal hygiene, the rationale is there.

Now, what about the overall effect of your garb? Assuming your garb isn't overalls, that is. (Sorry, I'm so weak.) Because my trade (writing) is often viewed as an aspect of homosexuality, I take care to dress straight and avoid disappointment. It doesn't seem to lure heterosexuals, either. But cats seem to like me, if only to play with my shoelace.

Anyhow, my favourite garb is shorts. They're quick to don, even quicker to drop, and I've been told I have good legs. The product of cycling hundreds of miles around the world. I don't flaunt them, mind you, crossing my knees in shorts and stuff. I just know that my knees are there, if I need a trump card in some sexual fantasy I haven't had lately.

Dishevelled. That is how a writer is supposed to look. Maybe it's tougher for female writers. I have no idea what they wear. Even though I am married to one.

So, as for me and clothes, I have more important matters to consider. What they are slips my mind for the moment. But I am sure they don't involve my having to wear a necktie.

HAIR TODAY, GONE TOMORROW

Gentlemen, let's face it: at some point in our life we are going to have to remove our hats. When engaged in sexual intercourse, for instance. Hat removal is also mandatory during the funeral of a loved one or a spouse, or during a job interview that you hope will lead to gainful employment. And, of course, at the barbershop. (Not to be confused with the hairdressing salon, where women let their hair down in rites occult to guys.)

Most of us males ignore our hair until it grows long enough to obscure our view of women. Or we have trouble locating our neck. My personal rationale for this procrastination is that people see me as a university professor. I may even carry a few books to heighten the illusion. I call it "the Albert Einstein Look." The Big Bang outweighs the little bangs. Bert and I have had no time to waste on personal grooming.

However, not everybody infers the too-busy-intellectual. The reason why I avoid standing at busy street corners is that I'm afraid someone will try to slip a quarter into my hand. It hasn't happened yet, but I have noticed near-sighted old ladies looking at me as though I may be selling pencils. (If my hand is out, it's just to check for rain, which is prevalent in our area.)

But, eventually, I have to attend the rites of a barbershop. And the barbershop in my area now has *a female barber*. A barberette. Thus the old pool table that nobody used is now gone. Replaced by a potted plant that smells different. No more venerable copies of *Playboy*. Instead, venerable issues of *Good Housekeeping*. An emasculated milieu.

And fool indeed is any male customer whose face invites a shave by a female barber without his first checking her dossier for unfortunate relationships with my ilk of gender. ("You have two ears,

sir. Do you want to try for one? Just let me tighten that tablecloth around your neck….")

Then there is the problem of conversation. *All* barbers talk to the customer, of course. They see it as part of the service, with major implications for the size of the tip. Encouraging the patron to express his views on various levels of government can goose the gratuity into folding money. But having a *female* barber can complicate the small talk. Which can never be too diminutive. The customer who allows his tongue to wander into topics other than the weather may emerge from the barbershop looking like one of the Three Stooges. (Curly?)

Also, with a gal barber, the questions tiptoe into one's mind: Is she smiling at me (via the mirror) because she finds me sexually attractive, or because she's massaging her tip? Possibly both?

Is she bibbing me to catch hair or drool?

And why am I suddenly hating my bald spot? After years of our ignoring each other. I suddenly miss my former barber, Andy, who had a bald spot bigger than mine and could run his fingers through my hair without my having to remind myself that I'm a married man

One time recently a lady barber actually produced *a vibrator*. I was only marginally relieved when she applied this sexually ambiguous device to my scalp. Where failure to respond is less devastating.

Despite the manifest hazards, I try not to let the imminence of a haircut bother my sleep. With my waking up bleating, "Figaro! Figaro! Figaro!"

Also, I have just recently discovered a barbershop that has four chairs manned — womaned? — by a bevy of Malaysian girls still learning the English language. I enjoy the seraglio ambiance, and for a measly ten bucks I avoid being taken for a bum.

HINTS FOR WITS

As a professional humorist, I have spent a lot of time — immeasurable thanks to unwound clocks — lying on my bed to create bonny *mots*. Some of my *mots* are bonnier than others. Especially if I doze off during composition. (One can't be expected to be both sociable *and* constantly alert for the timeless pun to pop into one's head, and draw one's own hearty chuckle that relatives interpret as dementia.)

Then, because of my dozing off (an essential phase of the creative process), I forget the memorable *mot*. I once tried keeping a notepad and pencil on my nightstand, to trap an epigram. But Morpheus, in whose arms I lie as favourite position, has no regard for *mots, bon* or otherwise.

Anyhow, one of the trusted criteria for professional humorists is that we are not smart dressers. Yet we try to distinguish ourselves from circus clowns by strapping on the putty nose only as a last resort. Otherwise we try to dress like normal people.

Attending university, I wrote a humour column for the student paper under an assumed name ("Jabez." Hebrew for "He will give pain.") I guess I hoped that the reader would rupture something, laughing. But the campus hospital never reported the hysteria victim I hoped for.

"He was born with a gift of laughter, and a sense that the world was mad." I forget who said that. It may have been me, but I'm not crazy enough to claim it. Nor do I try to exploit my passing resemblance to Robert Benchley (he, too, was a bit overweight). Benchley had the mien of a bloodhound with an ulcer. He appeared to take the audience laughter he induced as a personal affront.

Fred Allen was another barrel of phlegm. And who can forget the incomparable Buster Keaton? Who raised impassivity to new depths.

Having a reputation as a print humorist is a strong incentive to avoid a public appearance of *any* kind, other than appearing in court on a murder charge.

Socially, I have been severely impaired, I believe, by a reputation for hawking humour. There is a common belief that girls will do anything for a laugh. I have found this to be a dangerous — possibly lethal — myth.

I now try to avoid any social contact with more than one person, preferably an extraterrestrial.

In the past I expended too much creative energy on writing letters to friends, who couldn't be depended upon to save them for posterity. (Today, with email, God only knows how much priceless prose is being blithely deleted, by people I thought to be friends.)

As an alleged humorist, I make a point of being wry. "The loud laugh that spoke the vacant mind," to quote Oliver Goldsmith, sounds even more vacuous from one in my trade. Our professional mien should be much the same as that for a difficult bowel movement — i.e., comedy doesn't come easy.

In my forcibly humble opinion, people given to smiling just don't understand the situation. Let a smile be your umbrella, and howdy, pneumonia. Right?

HOW DECADENT CAN WE GET?

No question, we *are* living in loose times. Our Western culture is in moral decline. ("Decline" also means saying "No" — now seen as a negative attitude.)

Exhibit A: a plethora of sexually explicit movies and TV. More and more shows are prefaced with the warning: MAY NOT BE SUITABLE FOR CHILDREN. Which is why kids no longer need the gutter as a source of lewd learning. They can access the raunchy and the ribald in the comfort of their own house while their parents are out goggling at a film rated X, going on Y if not Z.

There is probably nothing much we can do about this seedy situation. Such periods of the overly permissive are cyclical, like El

Niño. Thus the temptation — one of the many available — is to just lie back and let the gamy tide roll over us. We may as well just accept the fact that our Western civilization is doomed to the fate of ancient Babylon ... Sodom ... Rome ... reincarnated as Vegas and some parts of Toronto (Bay Street).

The same seven deadly sins — sloth, pride, covetousness, gluttony, anger, lust, envy — are supplemented with the eighth (bad breath). To these damnable vices we may now add the fudge sundae.

Consider that major cultural force, the motion picture. There are people living today who remember when movies didn't need to be classified, for "explicit" material. The old western never had Tom Mix indulging in unnatural relations with his horse.

That relatively demure period known as Victorian was, of course, a reaction against the libertinism of the eighteenth century. (The first paved sidewalk got laid in London, 1765. Does this mean that our gamy twenty-first century will segue into a new era of the straitlaced? Holding society together, somehow, despite family ties hanging loose?

If so, what may we learn from Queen Victoria that got lost with Princess Di?

First, the societal limits that made life difficult for Oscar Wilde have been lost on the current generation, which seems to believe that sexual orientation is something imported from China.

Marriage is still an institution, but the fact that so many same-sex couples want to be put into an institution suggests a mental problem.

Other popular entertainment, too, has lost the aura of innocence. On TV, simple comedy has been replaced by the likes of mogul Donald Trump barking, "You're fired!" Which smacks of sadism, the staple of popular entertainment in Nero's Colosseum.

But it isn't "cool" to be outraged. When a female entertainer, one of the genetically bizarre Jackson family, had her breast bared as an unscheduled halftime event at the Super Bowl, millions of viewers made a point of not being shocked. The only protests came from football fanatics who saw the act as an abuse of the fumble. The umpire was remiss in not calling for a replay.

Such lapse into loosey-goosey moral standards has, of course, been exacerbated by that electronic den of vice: the Internet. Even the morally nimble person may easily stumble into the Web. The abode of salacious spiders, lurking to seize on any prey naive enough to believe they are safe from porn because they don't own a pornograph.

On the evidence, and deplorable though his means of making it may be, old Osama bin Laden did have a point in hiking around the mountains of Afghanistan instead of taking a taxi. The fanatic looks quite fit. And much as we may resent the intrusion into our comfortably decadent way of life, perhaps we should seriously consider whether having a long beard discourages lubricity. Perhaps because it tickles?

Whatever. Let us ask ourselves: Is there any way of our turning this gamy situation around, saving Western civilization from gurgling into the sink of iniquity?

It won't be easy. Much as we Canadians may see the value of dissociating ourselves from "the Great Satan" to the south, sooner or later we have to take off our ice skates. And that, it seems, is when we get into trouble.

Skiing, too, would at first blush appear to be a natural contraceptive. But research indicates that, while skiing may afford a temporary diversion from the slopes of hell, the moral temper of the ski resort is inimical to virginity once the planks come off.

In this state of moral decay, perhaps the best our wicked West can hope for is a fall into another grave depression. Economic, that is. Such as that of the Dirty Thirties. Those ten years of belt tightening helped to keep the pants on, morally. The flappers of the Roaring Twenties suddenly dropped their skirt length too long, matching the faces of the guys. And the all-too-free enterprise slipped under a grey cloud of socialism, as America's moral tone shifted from Belial to Boston in the person of FDR.

However, for the moment, the wages of sin are inflated. We Canadians can only cluck our disapproval of the era's loss of virtue, while we make no immediate plans to resurrect prohibition.

HOW TO SETTLE INDIAN LAND CLAIMS

(*This prospectus is offered to all levels of government, regardless of how low they have sunk*)

The best way to compensate the First Nations people for the loss of their land already exists: Indian-run casinos.

Same way that the white man acquired the Natives' territories by exchanging trinkets and beads and bits of copper, today the aboriginal-owned casinos are dealing out poker chips and playing cards to diddle the whites. Sitting Bull is now Sitting Pretty, thanks to a battery of one-armed bandits.

Sure as the Lord made little green lemons on slot machines, the white man will gamble away his property. All of it. Which is why the First Nations must be prepared to take care of the whites whose only possession is with the slots.

The likeliest scenario: the prosperous Natives set up the Department of Paleface Affairs. This department is run by a band member whom the chiefs consider to be unqualified to handle a more important portfolio of the aboriginal government, such as Wild Fish Culture.

Over time, the First Nations start to feel guilty about the degeneration of the white man, who is blowing his family support payments on Indian-run bingo. They invite a white people's representative to attend a national powwow. The chiefs listen politely, while smoking expensive cigars, as the Caucasian complains that white children are being conditioned to believe in the Great Spirit instead of Lotto 649.

To try to preserve the vestiges of white culture, the Native people agree to employ more whites in aboriginal industries such as gutting salmon and pacifying war canoes.

After a few decades of running their repossessed Canada, the Native people become more interested in the traditional medicine of the white man. Such as antibiotics. Some Natives experiment with pills prescribed by a white physician wearing the ceremonial mirror on his forehead and the symbolic forceps draped around his neck. The Natives often claim to feel better, after the rites, even though their eagle-feathers headdress has moulted.

Latterly, the Indians notice that their country has run out of timber, fish, and hockey players — staples of their economy. They trade the province of British Columbia to the United States in exchange for a vacant lot in Vegas. Their casino floor show features a stripper wearing a maple leaf.

KEEPING FAITH ON ICE

My believing in God seems less important than God believing in *me*. I have to believe that he — all right, He — does. After all, I am ninety. Indicating that God has seen no need to pull my plug, yet, on behalf of humankind.

Praying to God in time of need seems to me to be a tad utilitarian. In time of plenty, okay. No harm done. Way to go, Jehovah!

However, our intimacy with a divine power has been complicated a bit by astronomers confirming that our planet isn't special. Just one of thousands in a universe that is expanding faster than Dad's waistline. And there are untold numbers of other universes whirling around at a dizzying pace. Leaving no mind unboggled.

It is impossible to imagine what life forms have emerged on some of those planets. Probably not all human, though there may be a passing resemblance to Uncle Fred. Certainly, no Adam and Eve. (A nice couple, even though they never existed.)

The worst enemy of organized religion is the Hubble Telescope. Which has to be guarded night and day against religious extremists bent on blindfolding science.

With such a plenitude of planets, it is reasonable to assume that some of them have developed life forms advanced enough to be aware of *us*. But they haven't got in touch. Canny? Got a whiff of our civilization and decided it could be infectious? Possible.

However, it may be slightly less futile to speculate about just when — given the evidence that man evolved from the ape — did he acquire a soul? A sticky question that most people, wisely, choose to ignore. Does the ape have a rudimentary soul that at his demise goes to a simian paradise (bags of nuts)?

But that seems unfair to Rover. We all know the dog to be the soul of loyalty and devotion. To believe that he has less chance of sniffing the Gates of Heaven than does a customs agent violates our sense of fair play.

I do, however, believe that my militant skepticism has mellowed with old age. I no longer sneer at people — certainly not in labial fashion — who believe that their kneeling in prayer on Sunday morning will atone for their kicking up their heels on Saturday night.

I also believe that if a benevolent God had wanted me to kneel in prayer, he would have done something about my knees. Joints with restricted opening hours.

As for my transgressions, I am blessed in being unable to remember them. I know that I dodged "Thou shalt not kill," but there may be an extended list of sins of omission. I haven't seen it. And there is nothing like having a poor memory, after eighty, to make it easier to live with yourself, even if nobody else will.

Of course, if you're living with someone else, or plan to, and have reason to doubt your sanity, it may be time to consult a shrink. Just keep in mind that he or she is probably just as maladjusted as you are. Hell, nobody's perfect.

LIMPING DOWN MEMORY LANE

"You would forget your head," my mother used to chide me, "if it weren't screwed on." This idea, that my body was as unstable as a ketchup bottle cap, had no effect on my forgetfulness but did put me off the sauce for a time.

The elephant, we are told, never forgets. But does this improve the elephant's lifestyle? Isn't this animal subject to fits of temper, with environmental consequences more severe than anything tweaked by a piqued parrot?

Memory loss is associated with old age. It is nature's way of letting us forget how much we are now missing. Like sex, ski jumping, more sex. Recreation is pretty well limited to respiration — i.e., breathing in as well as out.

On the plus side, my short-term memory loss (STML) means that I don't hold a grudge long. A person can do me wrong without needing to be concerned about eventual retribution.

From my limited observation, I would say that men are more subject to STML than woman are. Woman never forget anything. Well, maybe their gloves. But no other clothing. If a guy's date greets him at the door wearing only black lingerie and spike heels, he may safely assume that it isn't her memory that has lapsed.

My wife has me on memory pills. I'd forget to take them without her. This may be why bachelors don't live as long as husbands. Whether that is an advantage is a matter worthy of inquiry by someone with more guts than this observer.

Apparently, there is no medication you can take to remind you to take your memory pill. Talk about a youth-oriented society!

"Did you remember to take your memory pill?" my wife asks to the detriment of a romantic dinner with a young wine.

"Yes!" I reply with alacrity remarkable for my age. "I did take my memory pill."

"Then what's that lying beside your plate?"

"Aha!" I cry. "A mystery pill! Closely resembling my memory pill, but obviously the work of the same evil force that put the towel in the toilet! If I catch the bounder ..."

"Take the pill," my wife advises.

My problem is that I have *long-term* memory. That is, I can remember anything that happened before the Second World War. My memory pretty much died with Hitler. Now, if I've remembered to zip my fly, I've had a good day.

But I do get a lot of exercise because of my gimpy memory. On my visit to the oculist who confirms that I am going blind — "visually impaired" — as a bat, I forget where I parked my car on one of several similar streets. From a distance, all parked cars look like my car. Because I've forgotten to take field glasses on the visit to the oculist, I'm obliged to trudge down the street, scrutinizing the parked cars in hope of recognizing one of them as mine.

This suspicious behaviour, observed by others on the street or in the shops, could, I know, get me reported to the police. Especially when I have to peer in a car window because the vehicle resembles mine by being red.

When my arthritic back starts screaming obscenities, I have to sit down on the curb until a passerby tosses a coin in my lap. Reminding me that I forgot to shave.

I have tried to think of my amnesia as a gift of nature, freeing me from recollection of all but the positive. This system worked fairly well until I ran out of good ideas.

To compensate for being mentally inclined toward the unkempt, I tell myself, "Remember Albert Einstein. We might not have the Theory of Relativity if Albert had got distracted by getting a haircut. Chances are, Einstein didn't smell too great, either."

Yes, this is rationalizing. The last refuge of the slob. However, despite its reputation as a pedestrian-friendly avenue, Memory Lane is full of potholes. For my good wife, who never forgets anything, it's a freeway. It's a talent that women have, to compensate for their child-bearing.

To conclude this piercing insight into the causes and effects of memory loss, I remind the reader that ... Damn, I seem to have forgotten a damn good summary.

As I may have said earlier in this diatribe, I can live with my forgetfulness. Whether anyone else can, well, I guess you'll have to ask my wife.

LONE RANGING

Attending the University of British Columbia, I rode a bicycle to campus. As a result, I was never invited to join a fraternity. I wasn't invited to join a sorority, either. The rich kids in automobiles saw me pedalling frantically to stay in the draft of a bus and knew that my pockets weren't deep enough to hold a party.

Today, from my study window, I see remarkably few neighbourhood kids riding bikes to school. They are being driven there by parents concerned about their safety. Actually, it is a form of child abuse because the kid's calves miss the chance to beef up, and the survival instinct gets flabby.

"I wandered lonely as a cloud / That floats on high o'er vales and hills," sang the poet Wordsworth. But it paid off in royalties. Certainly, travel is an effective way to avoid feeling lonely. There is always a helping hand. Waiting for a tip, maybe, but a quid pro quo is better than no quid at all.

There is a fine line between effective solitude and being seen as a hermit. Humans are social animals, and I classify myself as human unless I have had a really bad night. The owl may be able to hoot on his own, being wise enough to avoid public transit. But being limited to hooting would be a bind, at church. A housebound in-law of mine depends heavily on email for social intercourse. Email is certainly an advance over putting a message in a bottle and throwing it in the river. But email *is* a tad presumptuous. It assumes that the receiver's computer is in a good mood. (Mine sulks a lot, probably because I have dozed off while waiting for it to wake up. Anyone for jungle telegraph?)

Despite an earnest desire to be sociable, and besides having had a recent shower, I have learned from multiple decades of painful experience in social situations that speaking your mind can be a very honest way of getting yourself disliked. Howdy, hermit!

Now, it is generally recognized that the best way to avoid loneliness is to have a *relationship*. It may be a blood relationship, i.e., unavoidable, or a bloodless relationship, as with a dog that doesn't bite.

In earlier Western societies the cure for loneliness was to take a spouse. Holy deadlock. Today, with both spouses (spice?) working, the bonding is less secure than with Krazy Glue.

"Misery loves company," sayeth the adage. But this is probably not the best reason to join a golf club. Even though you spend much of your time in the woods, looking for a wayward golf ball. A bad relationship with golf balls can put you off dimples for life, so you miss out with cute girls, in favour of something stark-skinned.

"I wandered lonely as a cloud / That floats on high o'er vales and hills." Well, that can happen to a poet who doesn't shower at least once a week. Better you should join a golf club. You'll be alone in the woods, looking for your ball, long enough to compose an eloquent soliloquy. Addressed to whom it may concern.

MARGINAL PROGRESS REPORTS

This week's experience of physical intimacy: having my toenails cut by the podiatrist. A tense prelude of sitting in his waiting room with a half-dozen other folks having nothing in common but overgrown toenails. Not convivial.

I had the foresight to remove my socks, shocking my feet, which are rarely exposed to the light since I sleep socked. I observe my toes huddled together as if startled by the sudden exposure to the light. (On bath nights I am usually too busy being humiliated to be able to sit back and study my toes.) Damn it, they're cute! And completely unassuming.

Summoned and seated in the shearing shed, I am dealt with summarily by the podiatrist. He doesn't offer me the option of an anaesthetic. Instead he attacks my cringing toenails with the ferocity of a person contending with a heavy mortgage. Toenail chips fly like shrapnel. I could be blinded by my own feet. My toenails are proving to be the most durable part of my body.

I think if I were a podiatrist cutting people's toenails all day, I would have a drinking problem. But I don't smell liquor on his breath.

Anyhow, the podiatrist never looks me in the face. He wouldn't recognize me above the ankles. Nor I him below the bald spot. As relationships go, nothing to rate with the girls who made my toes curl.

MEA CULPA

Yes, milord, I am guilty as charged. I, too, have contributed to the emissions held responsible for global warming. I exhale *carbon dioxide*. I guess I could hold my breath more often by driving in highway traffic. But the car will still be exhaling the blanket of smog blamed for making Earth hot and bothered.

Because driving a car is a vital part of the global economy, by financing vital oil wells, I have to question the premise that global warming is bad for the Earth. It is certainly not reflected in the home gas bill — that is an effect of domestic warming. I can't be concerned about the polar bears running out of Arctic ice floes to jump off. Polar bears eat seals, whose flippers are one of our most reliable sources of applause. And applause is known to be the North's sole encouragement to live.

I admit I have done little to discourage the lumber industry from felling trees, which help to shade the Earth from global warming. I have a couple of trees on my home property, but they don't seem to have helped delay global warming. They would be more effective if I got rid of the house, I guess, but I'm not all that arboreal.

I do park my car in a garage that is part of the house, so that its emissions are reduced unless I start the engine.

Global warming is being blamed for change in the winter migration route of the admiral butterfly. The butterfly appears to be disoriented, flapping into Florida instead of less expensive digs in Central America and Mexico. Millions die en route because their navigation system has overheated. Global warming strikes again.

I curse myself for not seeing global warming coming. Until recently I wasn't even aware of it. As with nymphomania, I thought I'd been excused because of my age. Thus the temptation to ignore it. *Que sera, sera.*

Maybe global warming is going to be hard on our grandchildren. But luckily I have only one grandchild. I'm sorry that global warming may turn the Earth into a wasteland, but I am too old to ride a bicycle.

What scares me most about the effect of global warming on Canada is that it may make us susceptible to tropical disease. Like malaria and dengue fever. Until now I have never worried about our mosquitoes being the bearers of deadly diseases.

We all remember what happened to Humphrey Bogart when he was overtaken by tropical disease. His famous lisp got worse and finally died out altogether.

Global warming will also have a deleterious effect on Canadian women, whose high moral standards will be eroded by the need to wear scanty, revealing clothes instead of the ski pants and jackets that usually deter sexual intercourse, at least on the chair lift on the steeper slopes.

Scientists who have given the matter some thought suggest that global warming actually is a boon to mankind, as it makes it less of a shock when we die and go to hell.

However, even the Liberals don't support this rationale, believing that even the longest journey begins with a step on the gas.

I'll be very sorry if global warming affects the environment of penguins. I find comfort in seeing another creature that dresses formally and still looks awkward.

It may be that man will fail to adapt to global warming and will yield domination of the planet to a different, heat-loving species such as tarantulas. Well, such is evolution. You win some, as a species, and you lose some. We may as well enjoy the National Hockey League before they're next.

MIND OVER MATTER

How do you deal with your mother after you reach the age of puberty? (Note: the age of puberty varies with young people, so it may be difficult to tell whether you have reached it or not. Asking a policeman should be considered frivolous.)

However, puberty generally means being old enough to bear children, unless you are unbearable. Women bear children better than men because they wear an apron with pockets large enough to carry a weapon. They understand reproduction other than Xeroxing.

In this regard I was "a mother's boy," i.e., my mother doted on me. Especially after it was confirmed that she could have no more children by the usual route. I credit my present dotage to Mom. From her I learned the hard facts of survival, such as chewing food destined to be swallowed.

Because my mother was a beautiful woman, she attracted tradesmen in an era when maternal fealty was challenged by home delivery. From our backyard I watched tradesmen sashay into my mom's kitchen, and come out smiling as though they had received their tip in kind. I'm sure now that she played them like a hooked salmon. But at the time it aggravated my lust for firearms.

For whatever reason, most grown men displace their mother with a *wife*. They soon learn that today's model of wife is much harder to drive, or even park, than Grandma was. Grandma understood that marriage was the only way a woman could have legitimate grandchildren to spoil. Some parents never become grand at all, but go into politics, where the party games involve real money.

My female parent had a lively temper. "Here comes the Irish," my father would mutter when my mother was heaping her wrath on someone derelict in his duties. She came by her Celtic ferocity honestly. Her maiden name, Mannock, she shared with her cousin Mick Mannock, one of the Allies' most lethal fighter pilots in the First World War. I have studied Mannock's photo in histories of aerial warfare, looking for the resemblance that would justify me shooting people down if push comes to shove in the parking lot. But I have to admit that Mannock comes across as the more lethal.

And my father was an accountant. He did stand-up comedy, as well, when not in the Allied trenches of the First World War. I feel that I have made a career out of what should have been a lull between bombing raids.

Looking back on my relations with my mother, I would have to admit that I was tied to her apron strings for too long. It delayed my learning the facts of laundry. To the detriment of both my marriages. I learned the hard way that a mother's life is not necessarily altogether fulfilled by darning socks. This is why, when one of my socks springs a hole, I sneak the offender into the garbage can, i.e., my neighbour's garbage can.

As a retired mother's boy, I would warn young women to beware the potential husband whose mother has not been dead for at least twenty years. My message to guys is, if you have a living, attractive mother, *do not get married*. It will never work. Instead, get yourself a dog, hell, a goldfish. And treat your own mom with love and respect, at least once a month.

MY BROW HAS THE WRONG ATTITUDE

I subscribe to a couple of highbrow magazines. I may not read them, but I figure that it's worth the price just to impress the postman. You aren't going to get much respect from a letter carrier who deposits nothing but bills.

We owe it to the neighbourhood.

I keep the highbrow magazines beside my bed in case I need something to help me fall asleep. Some of them, like *National Geographic*, are picture books. I enjoy gazing at photos of places I don't have to go to. Most of them are parts of Africa, my favourite continent — as long as it stays where it is. I don't fancy this "continental shift" business, firmly believing as I do that the shift belongs on a woman. Who can go as far as she likes.

Thus most of my contact with raunchy pix has been restricted to the men's magazines I find at the barbershop. Since it isn't an assignation, I feel that I can't be blamed for picking up the magazine that is still damp from the previous customer.

How am I to know that this legal publication contains nudes? So it's named *Hooters*. Could be an automobile magazine.

The argument is becoming academic, anyhow, as more and more men's barbershops are owned and operated by women. The male barber, dear old Figaro, has moved on to more lucrative fields where he doesn't cut anything but corners. And female tonsorial artists provide only ancient *Reader's Digest*s and *Good Housekeeping*, which reminds the male customer that he has one thousand chores waiting at home.

Things don't get much better when I finally sift into the chair and the lady barber bibs me up. Will she try to burp me? Has she taken this job because she hates men — on the strength of an ill-fated affair with a guy who resembles me around the ears?

Not wanting to lose face with our postman, I only get to see a girlie magazine at the barbershop. Actually, buying one of these graphic publications would be a considered, deliberate act of voyeurism. Since I am thinning on top, so are my chances of admiring Miss Nude World 2006. (The barbershop is always behind a couple of years.)

It never occurs to me to buy a *Playboy* or the like. Cashiers are almost always women, who restrain their sneer only with effort.

So, a guy is pretty well restricted to a men's barbershop run by a lone male barber named Luigi.

Yes, yes, I have heard of the Internet. But I have yet to plumb the depths of iniquity. Which I understand are a murky region of depraved blogs lying in wait for the amateur creep.

To avoid the carnal temptations of the Internet, you have to be strong-willed. And that lets me out.

MY CAREER AS A VOYEUR

In my teens a major part of my physical fitness program consisted of walking back and forth in front of our local burlesque theatre. Undecided about going in. I was afraid that I might meet my mother coming out. Unlikely, but traumatic.

And I did have my excuse ready: as an amateur ornithologist I wanted to study the ostrich feathers comprising Gypsy Rose Lee's fan. Another naturalist question: Did Miss Lee actually perform in the buff? The question was responsible for the long queue of guys applying for a job as a stagehand.

My research into strippers was interrupted by the Second World War, which moved me into military bases well out of range of Sally Rand's balloon. However, my post-war education took me to the Sorbonne in Paris where I looked forward to being a resident student of the Folies Bergère. Both institutions proved to be a disappointment. As was the Windmill in London (varicose vanes). Both institutions catered to voyeur tourists, rather than serious students of erotic phenomena.

I returned to Canada still a virgin, my bursary wasted.

Today, as a happily married man, I have lost touch with just about any kind of prurient entertainment. I understand that strippers now work in bars, making love to poles and soliciting laps. This I consider to be a degradation of the ecdysiast art, which wasn't all that lofty to begin with.

I also refuse to go near one of our nudie beaches; there are less traumatic ways to be struck blind.

I am told that the titillations of burlesque are available on the Internet. But in that technocratic medium, what are the chances of an ostrich fan dysfunction? Also I suspect that Big Brother keeps tabs on Internet users who access Google to ogle.

Today there is a grey area between being a sex pervert and a subscriber to home entertainment. As for TV, a person can spend an entire evening stumbling onto something identified as adult entertainment. Voyeurism is *thrust* upon us, by golly, requiring a lightning draw of the remote, to avoid our being sucked into the pit of iniquity on channel 80.

For the same chaste reason, I avoid movies advertised as containing "explicit material." From what I have glimpsed of it — inadvertently, of course — explicit material is rarely stimulating if a person already has a bad back. Hardly ever is a naked human figure enhanced by good lighting. There is a reason why sexual desire is the only thing — mushrooms apart — that grows in the dark.

If all the world's peoples had fluorescent lighting, the overpopulation problem would wane at once.

Therefore I predict that — before you escape to the lobby for refreshments — Western society will be entering a new Victorian period of demure vestment for women. Men may not get the message for a generation or two, but eventually we will be back to wearing floor-length robes as nature intended.

As a factor in this mass disinclination to bare the body, Tim Hortons' doughnuts are simply too weighty to overcome for showing all. Instead we'll dress as ancient Greeks. But at least the ostrich gets a break.

MY DAILY FIX

"How do you manage to remain so mentally alert," people often ask me, "despite your advanced age?"

"Eh?" I reply without hesitation. Then I add, "Ah! My daily crossword puzzle! For me, solving the crossword puzzle is as important as my daily bowel movement. Without it I feel unfulfilled and cranky."

Which is true. I take my crossword puzzle book with me wherever I go — the doctor's waiting room, the ferry lineup, and of course the loo — because there is no better way of moving the mind in the direction of thought.

In a public place, being engrossed in solving a crossword puzzle is the ideal way to discourage other people — most of whom are unattractive and possibly emitting a virus — from trying to engage a person in conversation or other unprotected intercourse.

As a bonus, I may actually *solve* the crossword puzzle. That depends a lot on *the degree of difficulty of the puzzle.* Which is why I avoid the puzzles found in highbrow publications (those with print) such as the *New York Times.* Its puzzles are not my kind of masochism. I don't even understand the *answers* to some of these artsy-fartsy puzzles. Why go looking for mental depression when it's freely available from TV?

I also admit I wouldn't be able to solve even the most elementary crossword puzzle if I didn't have a sizable library of reference books — encyclopedias, atlases, dictionaries — the lifting of which from bookshelves constitutes most of my physical exercise program. My legs are no hell, but I have wrists of steel. Thanks to heavy consulting.

Despite these intellectual resources, I am sometimes — okay, often — stumped by the fiendish mind that has created the crossword puzzle. A registered sadist, this person, whom I picture as cackling in a spooky Bavarian castle, alone but for his or her humpbacked servant, Igor.

That mentally twisted genius creates crossword puzzles of varying degrees of challenge:

(a) difficult
(b) a lifetime work
(c) aw, sh–t!

It is a wicked mind that produces this drug, which is clearly addictive. If I don't get my daily fix of crossword puzzle, I become, well, in a word, cross. I desperately need reassurance that my brain, under the influence of passive vices like watching TV or reading comic books, hasn't turned to tapioca.

My thinking is that, once I have solved the crossword puzzle, I don't need to use my head for the rest of the day. It is free to collect dandruff or just keep my ears apart.

Is this addiction gender-specific? That is, are guys — and especially older guys — more likely to be hooked on crossword-puzzle-solving than are gals? From my observation of puzzle junkies stoned in public places, I conclude that it is a mostly male fix. Women appear to have something better to do, though it is hard to imagine what this could be. Just one of the many mysteries attending the gender.

For my own dalliance, I may be committed to the ultimate across and down: hell. Which I picture as a place not only uncomfortably warm ... but having all the crossword clues in Babel.

Bummer.

MY LOW SELF LIFE

I suffer from low self-esteem. (Well, I don't actually *suffer*. In fact, I take a quiet pride in my excessive modesty. Without flaunting it, that is, by walking around the mall half-naked, ringing a little bell and mumbling, "Unclean ... unclean.")

No, except for the need for a haircut, my displays of humility are purely verbal. And in this respect I think I am competitive with the Tibetan monk who is mortifying the flesh ... in moderation.

My self-esteem has never fully recovered from being a kid afflicted with rampant eczema. I had eczema on every part of my body normally visible to the public. Hands, legs, anywhere but private parts. I wore gloves indoors. Played goalkeeper in school soccer to avoid wearing shorts. Never learned to swim, an activity incompatible with being insulated by trousers.

I did grow out of that plague, but never gained the chutzpah needed for either public life or private life that involved taking off my gloves, let alone my pants. Instead I took refuge in writing, a solitary occupation that can be pursued fully clothed. Not *well* clothed, perhaps, but visibly clad.

The downside of being a writer with dry skin: I tend to fawn on people who can actually *do* something: the plumber … the auto mechanic … the gardener … I call my housecleaner "Excellency." Even if I know her name. Because she understands the anatomy of the vacuum cleaner.

I have tried to regard my low self-esteem (bad) as modesty that has put on too much weight. But I still bow to the postman.

Sometimes I wish I had a cerebral thermostat that measured hubris. Then my wife could read my eyes and say, "You need to top up your ego."

I have thought of owning a dog, as a reliable source of respect. But I'm afraid that shortly the dog would own *me*. Some breeds can quickly detect the lack of dominance in their owners, and there goes the toilet training. In no time my dog would be putting *me* out the door to tinkle.

As for having a cat, as a source of high regard: ho, ho. Every cat, alley or prize-winning Persian, knows that its credentials as a superior date back to ancient Egypt. It is part Sphinx. Which means your cat will still be eating real liver long after *your* dinner has degraded to dog food.

No, right now I'm thinking goldfish. A non-judgmental goldfish. That gapes at me with due respect.

MY PHOTO-OP FLOP

Seeking humility? Tired, are you, of being an ego-driven hedonist? Well, there are a number of ways to mortify the flesh: bedding down on nails … eating nothing but low-fat food … attending your kid's school band concert …

But none is as deflating as having one's driver's licence photo taken. This ordeal is particularly severe for the senior (me) who is under pressure to convince the authorities (aka bloody tyrants) that he shouldn't be taken off the road just because he can't see it anymore.

Hell, nobody's perfect.

But one's physical imperfections are precisely what the licence bureau camera is set to capture. Knowing this, from previous traumatic episodes, I expend a major effort to make myself look viable from the neck up. This cosmetic challenge starts with wearing a turtleneck sweater to hide the turkey neck — a sign of aging — from that ruthless lens.

I shave to remove any vestige of grey stubble and slap on baby lotion for whatever rejuvenating effect it may provide. But I have given up on applying makeup. I know, from studying my current driver's photo, that looking tight-lipped adds years to my mien, yet wearing lipstick could create other problems with the licence bureau clerk.

The unfortunate labial tightening occurs the moment I enter the driver's licence death chamber. The atmosphere isn't congenial. None of the staff appear to revel in their role in facilitating fatal accidents. Only the photographer looks relaxed, probably because she has been drinking before a day of shooting faces like mine.

First, however, like a gaffed fish, I have to be weighed and measured. This process establishes that I have shrunk shorter than on my present driver's licence, but weigh more. I am collapsing in on myself, a threat to other bodies in my orbit.

The photographer then instructs me to present my face to her camera. She does not say, "Smile!" I try to look vigilant and alert, but an ill-timed eye twitch records a wink that will be ill-taken by a cop.

"That's it," says the photographer, and I hate it when she crosses herself, as if feeling guilty about being instrumental in my driving. I am tempted to reassure her that any blood spilt from my driving will be my blood, as I drive a small car, without an attitude.

I am then sent to the licence bureau's cashier to be charged for this documentation of my decrepitude.

Later, in the mail, I receive my new driver's licence. I don't recognize the ghoul staring out of the plastic. Would I trust that freak to drive *my* car? No way! The authorities must have got my data mixed up with a coroner's report.

However, I guess I have to live with this travesty in my wallet. And it does encourage me to drive with extraordinary caution … if at all. I'm producing my driver's licence only over my dead body.

Meantime, I fear that the other ID cards in my wallet — library, bank, etc. — may gang up to expel that ghoulish driver's licence at the first opportunity. "Good riddance!" they will chorus.

Taxi!

MY SEX EDUCATION

A HORROR STORY

My sex education began at any early age. Five. It ended shortly afterward and did not pick up again until I was twenty. This may be why I remember the episode so clearly, in every horrendous detail: there was a long drought between my initiation into sexual intercourse and the renewal, a lamentably long time after I started to shave.

The locale for the first inroad on my virginity was East Vancouver in our lower-middle-class neighbourhood of houses set too close together to insulate a child from the facts of life. Our next-door neighbour was a family named Smythe, with a bewitching, socially skilled daughter — Lorraine. Lorraine was an older woman (six), and I was highly unsuspecting.

Thus I sometimes joined Lorraine and a couple of her little girl friends in her backyard to engage in games of tag or rope jumping. I was, in effect, just one of the girls, solely because of the dearth of neighbours with small boys who might have saved me from that traumatic episode, the memory of which still makes me — a senior — shiver and assume the fetal position.

"Let's play Doctor!" It was Lorraine who uttered this deadly exhortation on that fateful afternoon. Her friends endorsed her program, and I, a lamb to the slaughter, followed the medical team into the Smythe basement. Which became a hospital emergency ward faster than today's overburdened medical system can convert a linen closet into an OR.

"We have to take off his pants." It was Dr. Lorraine who ordered this procedure after a whispered conference with the attending physicians. For some reason, I didn't challenge this assessment. Instead I felt a novel excitement that blinded me to the fact that, despite the advances in ER treatment, no medical procedure is foolproof.

In a flash my shorts were jerked down and I was lying prone, giddily resigned to whatever heroic measures my surgical team might deem necessary.

It was then that we heard heavy footsteps descending the stairs from the kitchen above.

"It's my mom!" Dr. Lorraine didn't wait to close up. Instead, and in the blink of an eye, my medical team abandoned the operation, fleeing out the basement door. And the patient, with an instant recovery worthy of Lourdes, followed at a pace impeded by the struggle to pull up shorts and underwear while in rapid transit.

To describe this experience as somewhat traumatic would be like calling the sinking of the *Titanic* a boating mishap. The horror of that moment conditioned my entire social life, confining it to guys and *outdoor* games for years.

This, of course, seriously impaired my sex education. Observing the birds and the bees wasn't really enlightening for a kid with no impulse to build a nest. Also my sex education was impaired by the fact that I didn't smoke or drink — the two conventional means of knowing without understanding.

But my main source of ignorance was that, in those days, what kids learned about sex was picked up in the gutter. Our street was too poor to have a gutter. It had a ditch. Standing in which, a kid learned squat about sex.

Instead I assumed that a woman gave birth via the belly button. This was the only exit visible at the beach, which was my main venue for studying anatomy. And the evidence merely made me more nervous about the function of my own navel.

Apprehension became acute for me in the presence of girls, a situation made inevitable in the classroom of Langara Elementary School. My reaction to the proximity of a female never failed to entertain my classmates, especially when Brenda, the Grade 1 hoyden, took advantage of the teacher's temporary absence by leaving her seat to sit beside me. I can still hear the burst of hilarity this triggered as my face turned into a beet in heat. I'm sure it supplemented the school's heating system.

This was to become the prime curse of puberty for me: my blood was inordinately fond of my face as a display area. As a token of arousal, it was seriously misplaced.

At school I learned nothing about reproduction other than what happened in the mimeograph room.

Thus, as for the mechanics of sexual intercourse, the only guide I had for years was observing the performances of randy dogs. While I might be able to duplicate the tongue hanging out, the rest of canine co-ition left major gaps, in terms of approach. Also, *my* dog — a bull terrier named Spot — set a poor example by preferring to chase fire engines.

After I lost Spot to a ladder truck, my sex education became centred on our neighbourhood lending library. To which I cycled almost daily after school to browse in the fiction section. Ostensibly, I was checking out the westerns (Zane Grey) or the latest Charlie Chan mystery, but I also surreptitiously delved — with an interesting physical reaction — into the romantic novels, the bodice-rippers and bosom-heavers. Nothing as explicit as today's novels, of course, but still an inspiration to an adolescent engaged in hand-to-hand combat with pubescence. This exclusive relationship with books continued into university, the place where education is supposed to include sex, even if one isn't majoring in biology.

My major was French, but that still didn't liberate my libido. A non-drinker, depending on the bicycle for transportation, I was never invited to join a fraternity, the milieu considered to be most conducive to gender intercourse. Instead I was pressed into the French Club, meeting with some singularly academic females in a professor's home to listen to recorded Debussy. Nobody ever got relief from sexual tension by listening to "Clair de lune."

The intervention of the Second World War should have enhanced my sex education — we live for the moment, for tomorrow we die — but I never got to invade anything. Including women. As an airman subject to violent motion sickness, I became a terror weapon, bombing several Prairie provinces with the contents of my stomach. This affected my morale so severely that I had no heart for assaulting members of the Women's Division, and I became one of the few veterans to emerge from the war still a virgin.

Something had to be done. I was now twenty-six years old and had been gargling Listerine for years without progressing socially. I had also signed on for ballroom-dancing instruction as the first step to getting my arms around a girl. Faulty premise. At the very first lesson with an unconscionably attractive instructor, arousal kicked in. I abruptly abandoned the project. Because something had come up, unexpectedly.

Hence my seizing the chance to use my DVA benefit to pursue a doctorate at the University of Paris. Aside from the academic enhancement, I saw the City of Light as illuminating other research in the sexiest environment on the planet.

Bummer. My DVA handout didn't reach to my renting the private apartment in Montmartre that would have facilitated the kind of lubricious larking that helped to mature American novelists in the 1930s. Instead I was housed in a Cité Universitaire all-male dormitory where I developed an intimate relationship with bedbugs.

What my stint at the Sorbonne taught me was that the Folies Bergère isn't a true index of the moral standards of other Parisiennes. *Oui* is a word that buds the lips for a kiss, but I didn't hear it much. All I mounted was the Eiffel Tower.

That was why I abandoned my doctoral studies and moved to London where a Palladium showgirl took pity on my state of carnal innocence in exchange for babysitting her six-year-old daughter — the moppet from hell.

Thus my post-grad education abroad taught me that sex is a quid pro quo. And the pro may cost you more than a quid.

On the plus side, my record shows that I never got a girl knocked up, knocked down, or the victim of any other auto accident. For maybe too many years I was a good egg that never got laid. But on the evidence of today's overlaid society, I'd say that casual sex is an oxymoron — with the emphasis on the moron.

That is how I rationalize my sex-life horror story.

So much for the kind of sex education that makes ignorance look good. A horror story with a happy ending.

But, kids, don't try this at home.

MY WINDOW ON THE WORLD

Failure to wear a condom resulted in having to add a top floor to our family home. This work included a new bathroom in which I could take the cold shower I should have taken before I failed to use a condom. This bathroom was *mine,* all mine! Ablution nirvana!

The renovator installed a unique and ingenious bathroom window that the person using the bathroom could see *out* of, but that our neighbours — voyeurs to a man — could not see *into*. Not being an exhibitionist, except in print such as this, I admired my new bathroom window greatly, because I could safely ignore it. I didn't even wash it, leaving that lofty task to our cleaning lady, whose back is better adjusted to scaling walls.

Thus my new bathroom window and I lived happily together for several months before, one day, I had occasion to look out the window. Yikes. No see-through. Opacity defined. A glass wall.

I sat on the toilet to digest the horror of the implication. If I couldn't see *out* my two-way bathroom window, it meant that the installation had been as flawed as Hitler's decision to invade Russia. Like, the window was put in *backward*, thus inviting goggling spectators.

This analysis was confirmed the day that a roofer working outside the devious window looked in as I was contending with my occasional constipation, and he gave me the thumbs-up. It worked, but I failed to feel grateful.

And for the months that people — neighbours, telephone linemen, low-flying aircrew — had been able to see into my bathroom, I had attributed my neighbours' raucous laughter to their heavy drinking. Now I had to consider taking a bath as a sort of return of cut-rate vaudeville. I might even be included in some city sightseeing tours.

I also understood why so many of our neighbours' parties coincided with my trying to cut my toenails. Thus assuming various nude postures that Rodin wouldn't have found worth replicating. But the neighbours were probably charging admission. My bath nights would be a sellout. A lot of hooting and thigh slapping, as if there were something risible about a grown man bathing with his rubber duck.

These revelations convinced me of the need to give more attention to keeping a low profile in the loo. No loitering. I tried to think of my bathroom as the space station, subject to scrutiny by God and man.

More recently I have hired a different window company to replace my treacherous bathroom window with a pane that has glass warts, so that it cannot be seen through from *any* direction. This may be why neighbouring property values have slumped. I refuse to feel guilty. Those people still have television. And my ablution program *will* be available on the Internet at *rubbadub.com*.

NAVAL MANOEUVRES

One of life's little pleasures — rarely mentioned in entertainment magazines — is extracting one's belly button lint. A solitary diversion, yes, but more rewarding than watching television.

Umbilical excavation, as I call it, is one of the few private diversions not requiring a source of electricity. Any reasonably enterprising finger can liberate the abdominal orifice from the detritus which, if left unattended, may impair breathing. Not *your* breathing. Other people's respiration.

Odoriferous, it ain't.

And this characteristic mars the mystique of the midriff. Whose navel I, as a child, assumed to be the portal for the birth of a baby. I had seen no other likely egress. Thus I viewed my own navel with some apprehension. I certainly wasn't about to probe it, lest this trigger an infant that would distract my parents' attention.

So where does belly button lint come from? No one knows. Or, if the source *is* known to medical science, doctors are sworn not to discuss it. So we can only assume that belly button lint has the same genesis as ear wax. Which of course serves to protect our ear from invasion by earwigs. Why any bug would want to crawl into my navel, I can't imagine. But perverts abound in every species.

What *is* obvious is that the problem — if indeed it *is* a problem — originates with the custom of cutting the umbilical cord at birth. If the cord were left intact and allowed to, so to speak, wither on the vine, the aperture would be eliminated.

But I guess we would miss our belly button. I mean, it does help to break up the monotony of the abdomen. We can't imagine the Venus de Milo, for example, without the charming navel that makes us wonder who her mother was.

Yet what is visually attractive seems to collect rubbish that smells anything but divine. One hesitates to criticize evolution — which in other ways has been a positive development for mankind — but it does appear that our belly button lint might have been avoided if the mother human laid an egg, like the chicken.

Too late to hatch us now, of course. All a person can do is take a shower that includes power-vacuuming our belly button. A dicey procedure, as we are warned not to take the Hoover into the bathtub.

Note: if you're of the female gender and like to live dangerously, you may garnish your navel with a large ruby, sapphire, or other precious gem. This will discourage both lint and guys on low income. Just make sure that your tummy is insured.

NOSE ITEMS

I am very aware of my nose. Other guys worry about the size of a different appendage, but for me my nose has always been front and centre. It dominates my face, stealing attention from my eyes and mouth. Which have no opportunity to look sexy, lying as they do in the shadow of that monolith. Under which nothing grows. (I once tried to grow a moustache. Stillborn, because of that colossus that dominates my desolate lip.)

I can identify completely with Cyrano de Bergerac. When I read Rostand's play, I wept openly, thereby flooding the already taxed nasal flumes.

I avoid studio photographers, fearing that my nose in profile will test the peripheral scope of the camera. Chagrin for all concerned.

My relationship with my nose — a lifelong attachment — has afforded me ample opportunity to test the theory that, as we age, the nose is the last part of the body to lose sensitivity. A lifelong nervous Nellie is my nose. In elementary school I was humiliated by what was called hay fever. My classroom being nowhere near a farm, I felt persecuted by a rural bane.

I now know that sneezing and snotting are not dairy products but are set off by the simple act of breathing. Not an optional activity.

Neither was my going to school as a kid bulked up with a half-dozen handkerchiefs — a vain attempt to cope with the flooding schnoz. I still had to surreptitiously put the saturated linen on the classroom's steam radiator, creating a pestilent fog that may have been fatal for some of my fellow pupils.

Today, as a senior citizen, my nose remains as effusive as ever, having lost none of its capacity for hurricane-force sneezes and subsequent flooding that sends bystanders scrambling to higher ground.

Indeed, if anything, my allergy-born nasal holocaust has become more violent with age. I am a bit hurt to learn that some of my family members attribute the dust storms in China to my erupting proboscis.

I dread the day when age obliges me to take bus transport and watch dozens of panicky people scrambling off at a stop not of their choosing just to escape someone who is nasally lethal, and who is his own innocent victim. Brooding about ways to escape this domination by his honker (surgical removal would create a problem, as I wear glasses), I lack the talent to exploit my nose, as did Jimmy Durante. Who milked his nose for laughs.

At least I should try to see the value of a partition that keeps my mouth away from my eyes. "Your eyes are bigger than your mouth," my mother used to chide me when I overloaded my plate, but she never accused my nose of bad conduit.

My father, who had a sizable jib of his own, rarely looked at me directly at all, as if eye contact could make me sneeze and compromise our wall plaster. Okay, maybe I shouldn't look down my nose at my … *achoo!* Excuse me!

OH SOLO MIO

News headline: CANADIANS SPENDING MORE TIME IN SOLITUDE. Apparently, I have company in being a veteran loner. As kinships go, it's no heart-warmer. But I find it comforting to know that my isolation is a national trait rather than a failure to use the right bath soap. I have a lot of company, though not in my house, thanks.

I was a loner long before it became chic, as it now appears to be in this broad land. There is, however, no truth in the legend that at my birth my father said to my mother, "Let's call it Quits." I have never answered to Quits or anything like it.

I have managed to enjoy my solitude without resorting to more than a daily ration of email. A possible factor in my isolationist mindset: I have never slept with a woman. Or any other verbal form of life. I have, of course, been in bed with a woman. With the result of my having three adult children. But my switching from the double bed to a single in a different part of the house has curtailed reproduction.

Thus, the double bed has played no significant role in my life. My boudoir is furnished with twin beds, one of which I sleep in, the other serving as a repository for reading matter unsuitable for small children. Had I any (which I don't, to the benefit of *Playboy* and the pillow that provides security for my chocolate bars).

I can therefore vouch for the real benefits of solitude when taken in moderation. Number one: *introspection* — some people are terrified of letting their mind loose inside their head, their brain on idle. *Shallow* is the term often applied to these folks who prefer solitaire to bridge. Which is unkind, as it *is* possible to have messianic thoughts on the mount that flushes.

In worst-case solitude, a person starts talking to himself. This appears to be a harmless type of communication, unless he starts shouting, which can activate a landlord, if not the booby wagon.

However, he may create an *alter ego*, i.e., an alternative personality. This is probably better than having no personality at all. But the alter ego will not do your laundry. And may become animated enough to try to force *you* into the washing machine.

What is patently clear is that no Canadian should choose solitude just because a lot of other Canadians are opting to live alone. That is a morbid kind of togetherness, with no redeeming feature other than a budget saving on bath soap.

I suppose that I could organize some kind of group whose members never meet. The Society for the Prevention of Others. But we Canadians are already regarded by other people as rather cold fish, able to become passionate only on skates.

Now, about that story that Tibet's Dalai Lama keeps an apartment in Toronto. For times when he really wants to get away from it all ...

ON BEING A REFERRAL

It is a little-known fact: no one graduates from medical school without taking the Oath of Referral. Which, in part, states: "I do hereby swear, by the almighty Google, I shall leave no patient unreferred to a specialist."

This induces what is known as "a referred pain." In the posterior. A second given: whereas your family doctor has his office in your neighbourhood, accessible by normal means of transportation, your travelling to the specialist may require a passport. And a taxi. The latest taxis have no doors but sliding panels that oblige the ailing passenger to more or less vault into the back seat. If you don't need an operation before you go to the specialist, you will on arrival.

All cab drivers are trained to recognize any medical address as an emergency and will drive accordingly. They want to avoid having to clean up their cab after the passenger has been transferred to the hearse.

At the clinic the specialist is protected from patients by his *secretary*. Who has been chosen for the job because of her skill in operating the appointments ledger in which she fails to find the patient's name. If the patient is already having some doubts about his own existence, this interlude with the specialist's secretary should be enough to convince him that he is but a figment of his own imagination. If he ignores himself long enough, maybe he will go away. And good riddance, judging by the grimace on the face of the specialist's secretary.

"Please take a seat." The first prescription. "Just take an Aspirin" would be less time-consuming. But you join the seated horde waiting for specialists. You are waiting for your name to be called. If hearing is your problem, you must be ready to read the secretary's lips, or else become a permanent fixture in the waiting room.

Because all specialists run late, you may have forgotten your name by the time it is called. Check your driver's licence.

Summoned at last, you follow the secretary down the inner sanctum's avenue of tears to the examining room. "Just take a chair." You had been hoping to just take a pill, but no joy. "The doctor will be with you shortly." *Shortly* is med talk for a period of five minutes up to five weeks. Whichever, you have ample time to admire the decor of the examining room, none of which could be described as homey. In fact, the glorified cubicle is redolent of the *oubliette* of the medieval French prison system.

The specialist returns — hopefully during your lifetime — and opens your file without anaesthetic. You watch his face, tensed for the head shake and pursed lips that mean your symptoms are life-threatening, if not actually fatal.

He asks, "Have you had this problem before?"

"Yes, Doctor."

"Well, you've got it again."

The specialist then produces that ultimate therapeutic device: the prescription pad. On it he scrawls those occult symbols that make sense only to a trained pharmacist, or tea-leaf reader, before rushing off to a critical golf course. You are now cured of medical referral.

ON FURTHER EXCAVATION

I used to be aging like fine wine. Now, I am more like decomposing. I stay out of the alley the day the recycling truck comes through. It might reject me. I get enough of that stuff at my auto inspection.

In terms of aging with dignity, I probably complain more about physical ills than is compatible with stoicism. Everything is stiff except the upper lip. Which I tried to keep stiff until it interfered with my drinking. (I trust alcohol, as a painkiller, if taken internally. I don't know much about its use for athletic injuries, having identified the health hazard of exercising anything but my rights.)

I am fortunate in still having peerless eyesight. That is, I don't peer unless there is something worth looking at. Which can happen on some cable channels.

From my slouching position at my study window, I often observe a horde of people running in a good cause. I envy their mobility while resenting their intrusion on my conscience. As if I didn't have enough to feel guilty about!

On the plus side of personal fitness, I do take good care of my hands, as they are the source of my fingers. Without the fingers, I would have a lot of trouble scratching, which is a vital part of the literary composition by which you are even now enthralled. After an essay, my nose is a mess. A novel would skin me alive.

My legs have broken off their relationship with kneeling. I am saving my knees for prayer. My calves are cowed. So I am also looking for a religion in which devotion to God is expressed from a recliner. I see no need to mortify the flesh. It already looks totally mortified. As I am in encounters with a headwaiter.

Lately, I have been seeing a gerontologist. Not socially, of course. By appointment, which I put off as long as possible. I would sooner be seeing a pediatrician. But they seem to have an age limit, which I consider to be illegal.

I should, however, be grateful for having no more wet dreams. As a teenager, I had to consider wearing a diaper to bed. An idea rejected because of my need to find an excuse for later burning the diaper when I wasn't a smoker myself. Abstinence can be hell. It enhances sensitivity, maybe, but you can't take it to the bank.

However, the compensation is that as an elderly person I am less susceptible to blind rage. I can see perfectly, snit-wise. I am also blessed with having 20/20 hindsight.

ONE TEMP FITS ALL

"**C**ool!"
It is the most overworked, under-defined word on the teen tongue. The kids avoid the extremes of hot and cold. "Cool!" They verbalize sang-froid. A transfusion of aplomb more appropriate in us geezers.

To that younger generation, anything *cool* is excellent, except a reception.

Result: kids conversing sounds like a covey of hoot owls in heat.

Our youngster won't wear a warm sweater unless it's cool.

Driving a hot vehicle too fast is cool. (As, unfortunately, is the coroner's lab.)

For those of us of an older and, of course, wiser generation, the favoured word of approbation was *swell*. That swelling has subsided completely, with the medication of time. (How the word we associate with sexual arousal came to mean excellent isn't clear. Probably just as well; conjecture can say more about one's sexual aberrations than is worth risking.)

Then, after *swell*, there came the verbal regime of *neat*. This *neat* had nothing to do with tidiness, or undiluted liquor. Like *cool*, *neat* was a general term of approval. It had no relation to appearance any more than *cool* involves temperature. One of slang's little mysteries.

What *does* invite inquiry is the psychological significance of this vogue of an adjective describing a temperature that is neither hot nor cold. *Cool* suggests a temperate emotional climate. It expresses admiration for the insouciant. The apotheosis of the lukewarm.

The dominance of *cool* among our young folk suggests an aversion to display of emotion. (Which went out with Adolf Hitler.) It is cool to have the hots for someone, so long as the lust is kept in the fridge.

Yes, *cool* is about control. Admirable in our kids, but not to be overdone. As the old saw puts it, the person who keeps his head when all around him are losing it, may simply not understand the situation.

But what I fear most about the verbal dominance of *cool* is that it may somehow devalue ardour. Right now our kids are equating *cool* with excellence when, actually, the word works best with beer.

Keeping their cool is, of course, life-preserving for professional poker players. Or heart surgeons. But chronic cool-keeping may permanently damage a person's ability to muster credible indignation. Essential in Parliament and parental situations.

Okay, there is an element of envy in my aversion to rampant *cool*. Having difficulty keeping my aplomb in any situation resulting from getting out of bed, I lose — or at least misplace — my cool at the slightest provocation. I comfort myself with the belief that being *cool* depends largely on loss of sensation.

Or possibly a shortage of adrenalin. This feisty hormone — most apparent in guys — is what drives the will to win. It would be tragic if the concentration on what's *cool* affected such institutions as Parliament or the NHL.

However, the odds are that our younger generation will survive the glacial age, the dominion of "Cool!" With, perhaps, the timely assistance of global warming?

ONLY CHILDHOOD

An only child. Is there any advantage in being one? Or is it better to have a brother, or sister, or even an alter ego, so long as it doesn't try to borrow money from you?

I can answer this question, which otherwise might appear rhetorical, even discriminatory. Because *I was an only child myself.* Perhaps not meriting the italics, but a circumstance that killed any chance of my being an uncle, let alone an aunt. (My acting avuncular with the postman just seems to encourage him to toss my mail onto the porch from a safe distance.)

So, *why* am I an only child? I have found no evidence to confirm the family legend that my father, at my birth crib, said to my mother, "Let's call it Quits." Yes, some family documents do name me as "Eric Q. Nicol" But I insist that the Q is actually an O sticking its tongue out. A bit of a joker, my dad was.

Anyhow, here is the more important question: Is the only child at greater risk of becoming spoiled? Keeping the child in the fridge, when not needed for doing chores, invites matricide. Thus I was free to see myself as the centre of the known universe. I was spoiled rotten. Mine is not a Cinderella story. (I wouldn't know a cinder from a clinker.)

Since they had no other children, and the cat wasn't home much, my parents paid too great attention to my performance in school than was compatible with my becoming a juvenile delinquent, without their noticing. I felt obliged to become *an achiever*, regardless of whether this aggravated my hay fever.

When I won my first school diploma (for attendance, my best subject), my parents had it framed and put it on our mantelpiece, where it impressed upon me the importance of showing up. On time, if not before. If I can do something besides being there, I am having a good day.

Being an only child meant I didn't have to wear hand-me-down clothes. My short pants were bought new. Unfortunately, the Great Depression hit me below the waist, as my parents' income couldn't cover my knees. Luckily, my knees were dimpled, compensating somewhat for a face that was pimpled.

"I love your knees." I heard that remark from several flirty girls in high school. It bothered me because it suggested that nothing north of the knees was noteworthy. Sooner or later I would have to graduate to trousers or, worse, a monk's gown. And there went any chance of a sex life.

A larger grievance associated with being an only child: I became introverted. This went beyond relieving sexual tension by standing on my head, though that did seem to help. But I missed out on brotherhood. At university I never joined a fraternity, nor was I invited. I blamed this on riding a bike to the campus. I developed husky thighs, the social value of which was lost without the short pants.

Would I recommend your being an only child, if you have a choice? Absolutely. Best way to avoid sibling rivalry.

OTHER CAUSES FOR ALARM

Wheezing into my nineties, I check the newspaper obituaries every day to make sure my name isn't there. So far I've got lucky. Never mind that I may need new reading glasses. I still know a life sign when I see one.

What I *have* noticed is that most of us geezers hop the twig as victims of a little-understood plague.

We have "died of natural causes."

I never hear of a younger person dying "of natural causes." Youth seems to enjoy an equally natural immunity. A situation that I consider to be grossly unfair. I mean, today's kids are spoiled enough, surely, without their having automatic freedom from age-related arthritis.

If natural causes are the leading killer of seniors, I think we are entitled to know more about them. Are the relatives who provide the obituary notices for their elders simply *covering up an embarrassing cause of death?* VD, say. Or pickled liver, aka "natural causes."

In the absence of other research — and shame! I say on our university labs — I have been trying to identify these senior-killing "natural causes," so that older folk can avoid them. And the first located killer, lurking in virtually every home:

The ladder. This lethal object, its lair the closet or basement, just waits for the chance to be the last steps that Grandpa takes. The Stairway to Heaven is what the ladder is. It doesn't matter whether it is the extension ladder (which should never have been allowed off the fire engine), or the even more satanic stepladder, aka the Widow Maker.

In this category of deceptively inanimate objects that kill old people I would include *the garden rake.* That multi-fingered menace, lurking in sheds, waiting for the senior to step on it and receive a lethal blow to the face. Official cause of death: a stroke. A natural cause, of course. So the deadly rake gets off, scot-free, lurking to clobber the next senior incautious enough to go out to deal with fallen leaves.

Because police resources are strained, the medical examiners are reluctant to classify an older person's death as murder even if the body is found with a knife in its back. The codger obviously toppled into some cutlery when attacked by a natural cause of death.

One of the most popular natural causes we old folks die from is tobacco smoking. Cigarette manufacturers have long argued that it is mere coincidence that the two-pack-a-day lifetime smoker develops lung cancer — a natural cause of death for old people who have compromised their breathing by inhaling.

Luckily, I don't smoke, or play golf on courses where an elderly golfer, killed by a stray golf ball, will be said to have died of natural causes resulting from going outdoors.

Old people who drive automobiles are particularly prone to dying from natural causes. Car insurance corporations are very aware of this proclivity. They jack up the premiums. Just receiving notice of this extortion is enough to cause an older driver's blood pressure to soar to mortal height. Quietus by "natural cause."

Simplistic, that's what the diagnosis is. I'm thinking of the over-sixty-fiver who's banned from driving a car because his hearing is flawed, then gets killed trying to board a bus. No mention of this, in his obituary. Public transit — a natural cause of death for the oldster whose next of kin is his car.

One is forced to conclude that the media don't care what the elderly die from, so long as it isn't contagious. It certainly encourages the octogenarian to jump off a bridge. Let them try calling *that* "natural causes."

PERCHANCE TO DREAM ...

A nd experience *a nocturnal emission.*
It is, so far as I know, a subject not discussed in the school health lecture. A shame, this. Every night countless lads are waking from a sexy dream to find that they have fertilized their bed linen.

Unaware that this is a natural phenomenon, they feel tremendous guilt. Plus the angst of how to explain the situation to Mom when she retrieves the linen to launder it. And sees the ghastly evidence that her sweet little son has cast his seed upon the ground sheet.

And the lad sees the advantage of being raised by wolves. Near-sighted wolves.

His immediate problem — as I saw it on my first experience with the overflow from hell — is how to get rid of the damning evidence. Using your pencil eraser — totally futile. The rubber comes too late. The stain is merely expanded to become obvious to all but the clinically blind.

The original sin is compounded by the attempt to expunge it. Now, I can understand the difficulty of trying to include gender-specific yet vital information in the school health lecture, or as part of physical education. It would almost certainly exacerbate any drinking problem the teacher already had. (Compounding reluctance is the fact that an *orgasm* is often confused with an *organism*, which is something girls have, if *they* get unlucky in bed.)

Also unenlightening is the traditional parental lecture about the birds and the bees. Neither the male bird nor male bee is subject to an involuntary emission that soils the nest or hive.

So, is there any way for a young guy to avoid the sexy dream that drains his tank? Probably not. Dreams are notoriously difficult to censor, as the mind is taken over by the subconscious, a den of vice that is open for business the moment we fall asleep. And for a young guy with a lively libido, this means waking up in the Lake Country.

Another factor: unlike young girls, young guys don't have their period. They have 24/7 occasion to be mortified.

Are young girls subject to the nocturnal emission? If so, why is it not on the public record? Is Mother Nature guilty of gender discrimination here, along with girls' having to shave only their legs?

In any event, the feminist movement seems to have sidelined this particular aspect of sexual discrimination. More pertinent is the question: Should the parents of adolescent boys inform them — though not during dinner — of the possibility, if not probability, of their experiencing this dramatic effusion as a result of falling asleep? Especially if their son is already subject to insomnia?

Obviously not. This is one of the few situations where ignorance is bliss. As blisses go, it is quite short-term. But it is better to have had a wet dream than never to have loved at all.

In rare cases, the occurrence of a nocturnal emission may strengthen a young man's decision to enter the priesthood. Where its occurrence can be blamed on satanic forces. Which may be more effective, son, than wearing a jockstrap to bed. Where, sure as hell, your cup runneth.

PHARMACIST, HEAL THYSELF!

Since becoming a senior, I find my social life pretty much confined to people I meet in my local pharmacy. Most of them are pharmacists. Working at the drugstore that I inhabit as a second residence. I know most of them by name, because they wear an ID on their white jackets. And they know my name even before I hand them the latest prescription issued by my doctor. We are family, in a sick sort of way.

Thus I hold no medical secrets from my pharmacists. If I were on Viagra — which I swear I am not — my pharmacists would be the first to know. Even before my wife, who also enjoys a good laugh.

But I'm disturbed by the newspaper report that our pharmacies, in the frenzy of competition, are retrofitting their counters "to make them less intimidating." They are also training their pharmacists to "talk to customers instead of hiding behind high counters."

That scares the health out of me. For this customer, the high counter is my last line of defence. Right now I am unable to observe how the pharmacist is filling my prescription.

"Eye of newt, and toe of frog, / Wool of bat, and tongue of dog ..."

Okay, so pharmacology has improved since Macbeth's witches. I still like to be able to see if there's a peeved frog hopping mad back there, or a dog about to follow me home spitting blood.

What I *don't* care to see is the pharmacist crossing himself as he reads my prescription. Or triggering a trapdoor under my feet to expedite my exit with whatever venereal disease is indicated.

As for the lower counter making it easier for the pharmacist to talk to me, well, it depends on what he or she wants to talk about. If it is some instruction regarding the medicine, rattled off instead of his taking me on his knee and speaking to me, very slowly, I'm dead.

I also doubt that a lower counter will lessen the trauma associated with being summoned by a blaring PA announcement: "MR. NICOL, YOUR VIAGRA PRESCRIPTION IS READY!" Which attracts the hostility of other prescription customers, suspecting bribery, sexual favours, or similar inducement to prioritize response to my sordid need for antidote. Already I am wearing dark glasses and a scarf over my lower face to counter the publicity.

Another announced reform: a prescription is to be filled "in a matter of minutes." Now, this I welcome. In the past I have come to the prescription counter with enough provisions — food, water, etc. — to last a week. And I leave a note for next of kin to deter their dispatching a search party.

Drugstores are also promising to widen their aisles, which have been notorious for their forcibly reminding customers they are too

overweight to squeeze past one another in the aisle. And should be buying fat-reduction nostrums. My view on this: it is better to have squeezed down a drugstore aisle than to have had no sex life at all. (Note: I avoid the cold-remedies aisle unless I'm sniffly myself.)

However, if our drugstores are really serious about making their premises more customer-friendly, what they should do *is put in a bar*. If there is one place where a person would welcome the chance to sit down over a cold beer or a glass of wine, it's in that intimidating warren of woes, the drugstore.

No, alcohol isn't listed as a prescription drug, but it is known to be a superior painkiller, sedative, and all-round cure for the blues.

Go for it, Shoppers Drug Mart! Your pharmacists will never look better.

PHONEY EXCUSES

My phone rings. Ever eager to respond to anyone willing to talk to me vocally, rather than by email, I hustle to the blower. Hey, it could be Sally Forthright! The beautiful woman who has fallen in love with me on the strength of reading one of my books. Or possibly she saw me in the supermarket, palpating the plums …

But it's not Sally. It is someone who burbles, "Hello, Mr. Nichols. We're working in your area and can give you a special price on replacing your house with a modern prestige home …"

Now, if I were contemplating getting rid of my dwelling, this call might be seen as providential. But I am not. Thus it rates as a pain in the rectum. And I hang up. Hard. I know that the vehemence is lost on the telephone pole in the lane, but I find some satisfaction in aggravating the arthritis in my wrist.

As visible testament to the vehemence of my response to this genre of phone call, my phone cradle is swathed in tape and the receiver appears to have been bitten, though I don't recall the occasion of my being provoked enough to masticate the miscreant.

Televendors seem to be fewer, however, since I started answering the call — "Good afternoon, Mr. Niggle. How are you?" — with "Oh, thank God you asked! I've been feeling suicidal because of this terrible pain in my ass …"

That invokes the quickest hang-up since Alex Bell invented the wretch.

In deference to my arthritic hinges, namely knees that resent any pace faster than the polar ice melt, my wife bought me a remote-control blower that I can carry in a holster and draw if threatened with communication.

The main drawback to this method of receiving phone calls is that it is a constant reminder that I am not getting any. For a while I blamed this on the battery. Which apparently had the lifespan of the cabbage moth.

My phone has an idiot companion: the answering machine. Its red eye stares at me accusingly. Never blinking. My fantasy of earlier days — that someone phoned me while I was out — is defunct. My answering machine is now an archive for phone messages I would sooner forget.

Would it help production of incomings you ask if I made more outgoings? Possibly. But it seems like a shaky basis for a relationship if you have no real friends. Emailing them is the safest way to communicate. You should try to supplement your emails with funny stories. (If you don't know any funny stories, these may be purchased online from a reputable jokesmith.)

I do not — need I say — own a cellphone. Reason: a cellphone isn't compatible with a person who suffers from hay fever. My pockets are fully committed to handkerchiefs needed to stem the nasal Niagara. And I can't imagine the value of carrying around a constant reminder that nobody wants to talk to me.

Now I'm going outside to check for smoke signals. It's a long shot, but there's no service charge.

PORE ADVICE

This is a public service message. It is vital to see your pores — those smaller openings in your body — as *the sewers of your skin*. If you have ever studied an ordinary street sewer, you may have noticed that it can collect a lot of rubbish that was unable to exit through the grille, even though your wallet accomplished that feat after your grad dance.

Okay, so how do you purge your *skin* sewers? Vital question! Yet you may never have given this serious thought, being too busy slapping on the sun lotion or deodorant that only aggravates pore stress. Well, shame on you! However, it may be not too late to save your skin. Help is, literally, at hand. My own non-patented solution for poor pores: *scratching!* I have a long record of scratching. I have scratched just about every skin surface of my body that I can reach without getting into a spasm that is hard to explain to Emergency.

As a creative writer, I can personally attest to the value of scratching. You see, creativity is highly dependent on this measure. It is the physical manifestation of *reflection*. Looking at yourself in the mirror will do nothing for your skin. Except maybe make it crawl. Not beneficial.

One reason why I have never embarked on writing a novel is that I know that the amount of musing involved would result in complete dermal catastrophe. There is no point in accepting the Nobel Prize for literature if you have to wear a hood.

On the positive side, I credit my scratching with my having a schoolgirl complexion. The girl has gone to reform school, but no one is perfect.

Now, some writers divert their attention from work by doodling. I have never been able to doodle effectively. I get nagged by conscience, going on about the cost of living, the advantages of affording food, niggles like that. But nothing to interfere with my scratching.

To try to divert attention from my nose, I have tried writing in the nude. Just to expand the scratchable area. But my belly isn't firm enough to satisfy my nails. The washboard has gone jelly roll. A tactile flop.

To summarize: I consider it regrettable that college courses in creative writing don't include at least one lecture on skin care. Instead they send kids into the world without a word of warning about what even an essay can do to your nose. A novel, complete depilation.

The Chinese Mandarins, being wise old coots, never cut their nails. It testified that they were above manual work. But when I try it, my wife chides me, even if I'm walking around in a bathrobe.

I have been told that I can both purge my pores and save my skin by taking a steam bath. But steam baths are known to leave you in a grubby relationship. I can get that cheaper at the Y.

The bottom line: scratching is less pernicious than watching daytime television. But doing both: deadly.

POSTERIOR INSULATION, INC.

Let *us* cover your ass for you! Why waste your precious time making excuses for something disgusting you happen to have done? Or not done? A grey area that can turn black unless you *act now* to escape criticism and a possible jail term. First, our trained technician will convince you that *your brain is not to blame for what you have been thinking*! But you do need to *act now* to escape criticism that can permanently damage your self-esteem and cause terminal cheek twitch.

Now, before we insulate *your* ass we must first establish that it is not your *mind* that is vulnerable to feelings of guilt just because you happen to have done something despicable. Commit it to memory: *nothing you have done is your FAULT!*

No matter how grave or disgusting your error may have been, from committing murder down to farting in company, the faux pas can be blamed on environmental change (global warming), plus factors in your childhood and even prenatal conditions, such as your mother having worked in a car wash.

Was your father involved in politics? Especially federal politics? (Ottawa is widely recognized to be the ass-covering capital of the country. Children exposed to the atmosphere of the capital are likely to suffer damage to their ability to distinguish right from wrong without the assistance of a public relations officer.)

Other causes of moral apprehension are well-known:

- Your boss has discovered that you have been stealing paper clips and sexually molesting his secretary (temporary dementia).
- You forgot that it was your spouse's birthday (fourth year in a row: chronic dementia).
- You have been medically diagnosed as infected with a sexually transmitted disease (result of using a public toilet).
- You strongly suspect that you are a coward, possibly craven.
- You relate to the Yellow Pages of the phone book, which you find more understanding than the heating bill.

Don't let these niggling matters of conscience impair your freedom to make bad choices!

Enjoy the bliss of knowing — thanks to POSTERIOR INSULA-TION — that your misdemeanours are fully covered! *Phone now* to make an appointment to talk to one of our professional, fully registered apologists, who will come to your home and explain how, for a few hundred dollars a month, *you, too,* can play with fire without taking the heat!

Note: most of our trained posterior insulators are former public-relations officers, fully experienced in padding accounts.

REQUIEM FOR A SCRIBBLER

Dearly beloved, we are gathered here today to offer a eulogy for a lost art: handwriting.

Yes, I refer to that venerable method of messaging by pen or pencil. The graphology snuffed out by the computer — by no means the least grievous crime committed by that soulless processor of words.

A reverence for penmanship was, in my school days, bonded into my spirit, thanks to my being evangelized by the MacLean System, the holographic equivalent of the *Kama Sutra*. (I never met the mighty MacLean myself, but pictured him as a sternly kilted Scot who lashed out with his cane to correct any kid whose handwriting failed to duplicate the script he mandated.)

I also had the example of my mother's handwriting, which reflected the genteel English environment of her childhood, as well as her running away from boarding school, never to see her parents again. All of which one found in her feisty curlicues.

In contrast, my accountant father, a waif whose unidentified sire was a travelling man, wrote a tight, terse script devoid of furbelows. Neither parent had any relations with a computer, probably a factor in their living into their nineties.

Now the day is coming — if not already here — when high-tech man is unable even to write his name *without* a computer. His laptop no longer a living secretary. Bleak company indeed.

Meantime, the popularity of graffiti suggests there is a longing for handwriting, even though restricted to building walls and one-syllable words. "F–k you!" — writ large — conveys more exhortation than the same words transmitted by email.

As script, email is sterile. But the prime advantage of the pen or pencil is that its very form reflects character. You can judge nothing about the sender's true nature from his or her email. Furthermore, a blackguard may blog without giving a hint of the evil that lurks in his heart and would be evident if he scribed the letter *y* without its appendage (whereby hangs a tale).

But the pencil! What an amazing writing tool! If people had been using the computer since God was a pup, and we were introduced to this new device, *the pencil*, what delight we would find in the tactile pleasure of actually creating words *with one hand*! Words whose unique formation says more about one's character than a person would care to reveal! Living on the edge!

Yes, the pencil gets personal. Like the bullet, it lives on lead not spam. They have yet to invent a laptop you can park behind your ear. Nor can you chew its eraser as part of the creative process.

But we face creating a generation that is unable to write *anything* if the electricity is off. Doomed is the castaway on the sand beach of a South Pacific isle, the fur trapper lost in the snow on which he is unable to tramp *help!*

Already we have a generation of school kids who can't exchange notes in class without assistance from Google.

Therefore, Bill Gates be damned! And *vive* our trusty Faber HB!

QUAKER SPIRIT

I live on the Rim of Fire, i.e., one of those lands encircling the Pacific Ocean — Japan, Russia, Alaska, British Columbia, California — known to have all hell ready to break loose under our feet. Without giving a week's notice. Earthquake!

Yes, it's exciting. An excellent excuse to live for the moment. Yet most of us drive as though we were homing in on the Prairies. Okay, if I'm having a normal dull day, I may remind myself that at any moment my house could start jittering about on its foundation. Earthquake! Who needs New York City for excitement when one is living on the brink of disaster?

True, Florida has its hurricanes. But that's just flatulence. Miami is all wind and no movement. I have that every day.

The West Coast is where the real action is. Maybe not today or this week or even this year. But *some* day all hell is going to break loose, and I am going to be on the TV news, dramatically clad in rubble, to recount how I held up the wall of our local kindergarten long enough for the bigger kids to escape.

Oh, yes, it will be a *major* earthquake. My insurance claim will include not only the loss of our house but the aggravation of my hay fever.

Sometimes, in bed, at night, I think I can hear the tectonic plates grinding against one another. It turns out to be just my teeth. But some night, or day, for sure, the eyes of the world will be turned in awe at both the titanic forces of nature and my personal demonstration of the gritty strength of the human spirit, despite the loss of cable TV.

Meantime, I have an excellent excuse to postpone our home improvements — all of which involve my doing work — in light of the fact that the whole structure is due to be toppled into the street, or where the street was.

Long-term planning, I call it. And I am constantly annoyed by the short-sightedness of neighbours paving driveways and walks that will be cracked and heaved as early as next week.

Yet we are ready, at our house, for the Big One, i.e. the shaking that registers whopper on the Richter scale. (I've never met Richter personally, but he sounds German, and those people are known to be sensitive to the Earth's movement.) And I am constantly on the alert for signs of prelude to the Big One:

1. The cat leaves town. (At the moment we don't have a cat. But I am alert to the unusual behaviour of neighbour cats, dogs, and gazebos.)
2. I hear rumbling that doesn't seem to be related to my digestive system.
3. My broker, Slim Pickens, can't be blamed for the shock waves.

Pending our Armageddon, I have posted IN CASE OF EARTHQUAKE RULES in our front hall as a service to visitors.

1. GET OUT OF THE HOUSE!
2. STAY WHERE YOU ARE IN THE HOUSE UNLESS THE HOUSE IS TRYING TO GET OUT OF THE LOT.
3. THE OWNER WILL ACCEPT ANY REASONABLE OFFER FOR THE HOUSE.

If you're unable to move your house before it moves you, at least stay away from windows, doors, walls, ceiling, and floor. *Think float.*

Meantime, I shall be hoping if not praying that the Ring of Fire turns clinker. By next Friday would be nice.

SCRIPT TEASE

Newspaper headline: COMPUTER USE POWERS BETTER WRITING SKILLS.

Well, maybe so. But not in my experience. For me, computer use powers my swearing skills. I've learned several new words and phrases — none of them publishable — thanks to my computer.

That is why this piece is being written first in longhand. With a low-tech pencil. A study in obsolescence. You, dear reader, may not be old enough to remember the pencil. Well, without going into leaden detail (ha-ha), the pencil was a pen with a *cil*. It was usually more portable than a laptop. Often carried behind the ear — a visible token of literacy.

Anyhow, this story elaborates on the writing virtues of the laptop, citing a group of British Columbia school students whose English scores improved by 30 percent, thanks to Bill Gates.

I fear that this technological triumph spells the demise of handwriting, buried under the avalanche of email. Surviving only as crude notes taped to the fridge.

A pity, this. Me being old enough to have suffered through elementary school periods of instruction in the MacLean System of handwriting. Now, computer illiterate, I am stuck with an antique method of communication. Hunt and pecking my way to a reader. Lotsa luck, Pops.

However, I have a more general concern about the evolutionary dominance of the laptop. Beyond the fear of its creating sexual impotence in males. The concern is this: *handwriting says more about the writer than the words it creates.*

It is involuntary revelation. The best kind! Perhaps not one that the mature writer would choose. But, for the reader, what

revelation of character lies in the way his words' letters lean forward (bespeaking a spunky nature), or his putting tippy tops on his *t*'s (emotionally insecure).

I'm not sure what *my* handwriting says about me, but I suspect that this ignorance is, if not bliss, benign. My script certainly lacks the generous aspect of my mother's, with its curlicue capitals. My father's hand was graphically constipated (no loose vowels), as he was an accountant by trade.

Nobody in the family has written with the visual eloquence of Shakespeare, whose surviving personal documents (mostly legal) verify the flowering of the English language in his time. Can we imagine anything so elegant, so glorious, had Shakespeare written his plays on a laptop? (First, he would have to get rid of the email spam. Which might put him in a mood to write *Richard III*, but we could forget about *Romeo and Juliet*.)

It is my firm belief that a writer should put nothing on top of his lap except a secretary. If she looks creative.

Yes, the piece you are now reading was first written in longhand before my being obliged to transplant it in the computer — a delicate operation during which it could die. I am much more comfortable writing out our household shopping list. In longhand.

And really making a meal of *marzipan*.

SEX, THE FOUR-LETTER WORD

My sex education got stuck in elementary. During my formative years (thirteen to fifty), my sex life was competitive with that of Mary, Queen of Scots. I was like a branch of the virgin forest. Nurtured by the ignorance of the confirmed dork.

Once, in my twenties, driving home late one night from a Writers' Union meeting, I saw a shapely young woman standing on a street corner. Knowing that the buses had ceased running in that area, I stopped and picked her up. She slid into the front seat beside me as though quite familiar with the make of auto I was operating.

"Where can I drop you off?" I asked my passenger.

The question seemed to faze her. She asked, "Where are you going?"

"Home. Do you live in the neighbourhood?"

"No," she said. "You can let me out here."

Since I had driven only a few blocks, I had to wonder why this young woman hadn't walked the distance. She certainly had the legs for a toddle, if she took off the spike heels.

But I just said, "Sure," and stopped the car to watch her scramble out. "Have a nice evening," I said without drawing a reply.

Driving on, I saw in the rearview mirror that the young lady was lounging on the street corner, as before, but scowling as though it wasn't her first choice as a place to solicit business.

Then the penny dropped. That nice-looking girl was a *hooker*! She had hooked *me*. And thrown me back. For being under the legal savvy.

Another time, with the hormones humming loud enough to confound common sense, I asked a worldly fellow university student to introduce me to a loose woman who wasn't majoring in commerce. He escorted me, by moonlight, to the yard of an east side rooming house, in whose shadow he introduced me to a hastily-painted lady in a dispirited wrapper, the contents of which were difficult to assess.

I shoved a twenty dollar bill into her hand, and ran.

Thus I lost money and a friend, without gaining any measurable relief from sexual tension.

Later in my career as a non-gay Lothario I accepted a bursary to pursue a post-graduate degree at the Sorbonne in the Left Bank, a reliable place to deposit your virginity. There I could study streetwalkers who actually walked the street, with a hip movement calculated to divert attention from Baudelaire's tomb. Hiring one would have furthered my education, but the bursary didn't cover it.

Linguistically, however, I learned a good deal about female body language, which in France is much more evolved than in Canadian towns. Where women are apt to think that walking fast is the quickest way to get somewhere. Without wheels, that is.

From Paris I moved my lack of sexual education to London, where being a virgin, at my age, was still less of an anomaly. The British were looking for an excuse to have wild sex without the threat of an aerial bomb attack. It was before the Python era when I might have absorbed the full Monty. As it was, I had no intercourse protection except working for the BBC.

Unfortunately, I fell in love with an upper-class English blonde who drew a line in the sand that stretched all the way to Dover beach. I returned to Canada a sadder, if not wiser, monk.

Today I don't remember *where* I lost my virginity. I may have just mislaid it. While under the influence of marriage. Though this premise is weakened by my having three adult children.

Ain't life gland?

SEXLESS IN SPACE

NASA has announced that spacecraft travel doesn't lend itself to sexual intercourse. Just how the space agency discovered this drawback to extraterrestrial voyage isn't disclosed, but the caveat has cast a pall over Houston.

Yet to date we have read no report of astronauts defying weightlessness by having a sex party and to hell with worrying about bouncing the space station out of orbit.

We have assumed that astronauts are selected only after intense screening designed to detect chronic libido, or even occasional bouts of lust for something other than glory. It's why Canadians are favoured for astronaut training: in a spacecraft they will be distracted by nothing but a hockey puck. They match the stamp of the early Christian monks who traipsed around medieval Europe to set up monasteries as pit stops to Heaven.

It may help if we think of our astronauts as the anchorites of tomorrow. It being a lot cheaper to equip a spacecraft with a bed of nails than with a travel-agency-approved play mattress.

Meantime, NASA's bulletin is bound to put a damper on plans of other people hoping to holiday in orbit. Spatial ecstasy is now pretty well restricted to the Stairway to Heaven.

So why does weightlessness restrict whoopee? Answer: the gravity of the situation isn't compatible with the missionary position. The natural force that attracts one body to another becomes bad for both bodies if they are ricocheting around inside a rocket.

This hazard means that vacationers hoping to get a visa to visit Venus may have to fill out a form that includes the question: "Do you expect to have sex before you return to Earth?"

After watching years of *Star Trek*, whose characters had sex all over the known universe without having to wear weighted boots, we find no joy in being Earthy. Instead we have to envy our earlier explorers of planet Earth. Like lucky old Captain James Cook, who could invite Pacific island native girls aboard ship for research without having to worry about creating a shock wave that imperilled his craft.

All in all, space travel is shaping up as a bit of a drag. Not really competitive with a tour around Vegas. Unless, of course, Venus proves to have a truly spectacular floor show.

SO, EMAIL

A s a method of messaging, email represents an advance over the smoke sig-
nal. Which, of course, was restricted to the outdoors. Other advantages are more obscure. It may not, for instance, be good for civilization that we now start our day, every day, with the ritual known as
"checking our email." Right up there with the matutinal bowel movement (which it resembles in other ways also) is this routine. It has
largely replaced the morning prayer, as we pay homage to Bill Gates.

This email ritual helps to confirm our belief that we are still alive.
Someone outside earshot has included us in their attention, though this
may be shared with a number of other organisms, including humans.

The downside of email — aside from its being prostitution of the
telephone line — is that it reveals little about the sender's true character.
Romeo had to stand under Juliet's balcony, possibly in the rain, in order
to convey the message for which today's suitor merely hits *send*. And
Juliet can *reply* without even having to comb her hair first.

This facility is truly facile.

In contrast, the script as created by hand has said a lot about the
sender's character, whether or not he or she would prefer not to blab
the significance of the letter's slant, the undotted *i*, the flamed caps.

Here are just a few of the other ills of email, none of them
terminal but all of them diminishing the meaning of life.

1. We can tell nothing from how the email we receive smells.
   It is impossible to send a scented email. What a loss,
   compared to the very special aroma of the love letters of
   old! Okay, it's a break for hay fever sufferers. For normal
   noses, however, a treat lay in the lavender-emitting love

letter, or the manly miasma of the reply penned by a guy breathing brandy.

2. Besides being odourless, email is dumb. It has no voice. It is impossible to be sarcastic, for instance, by email. Irony dies on the vine.

3. Even when double-spaced, email doesn't facilitate our ability to read between the lines.

4. In its tiny, literal mind, email believes that no pun should go unpunished. It has the soul of a railway schedule. Any deviation is sternly derailed to the Internet, where it is blogged and made available to millions of parrots.

5. Finally, email is entirely dependant on the temper and disposition of a computer. Probably the most temperamental imp ever devised by Satan's tech team. The computer never forgets and never forgives. It is easier to get rid of a wad of gum stuck on the side of your shoe than to scrub the slate clean of the regrettable, libellous email you sent to the Letters to the Editor.

Switch to carrier pigeon. You'll still see some shit, but you won't have it in your office.

SOBER THOUGHTS

Damn it, I fear I'm going to snuff the wick, hop the twig, masticate the dust, without ever having been part of a drunken orgy. Truth to tell, I haven't even participated in a *sober* orgy. Now, for a senior citizen and grandfather, the chances don't look good that I shall be included in any kind of orgiastic occasion. Unless, of course, my Grey Cup really runneth over.

With a debauchless record like that, I shall be cheesed to land up in hell, anyway. I've been hoping to have my sentence of eternal damnation reduced to shorter-term perdition. Served in some minor-league Hades resembling Ottawa.

Otherwise, I'm going to be incontinently peed off, even bitter, about having missed out on being part of a social occasion where my making a fool of myself was in tone with the group dynamics. Result: I cannot recall my ever having been part of any really entertaining debauchery. Instead, I recall numerous austere gatherings at which I never let my hair down, let alone my pants.

Why? Well, for one thing, I don't ski. Never have. The one time I tried to ski I had to be rescued by a ski patrol. And I was still hanging on to the ski lift. Which means that I have missed the après-ski parties that are said to be partly responsible for the melting of the polar ice caps, and with it global warming.

Nor have I ever been able to afford to buy a yacht, which I believe is a popular milieu for a drunken orgy. More than the sails are said to be three sheets to the wind. I haven't even been invited aboard anyone *else's* yacht. Yacht owners sense that I don't roister well. Or somehow word has got around that I don't know how to swim. Meaning that someone else at the orgy would have to rescue me when I wandered overboard.

Unable to either swim or ski, my opportunities to participate in a Lucullan banquet have been severely lacking. I suspect that word has got around that I am not the life of the party. On the contrary, I can be the death of the party. I have watched more than one social affair go into cardiac arrest just minutes after I make an appearance.

Could I have a drunken orgy by myself? Not according to my *Oxford Dictionary*, which states flatly that an orgy is "a wild festivity esp. with much drinking and indiscriminate sexual activity." It is pretty hard to have a one-man festival unless you are drunk enough not to notice you are flying solo.

But what really disturbs me is that, in the course of a long life lived in urban centres, with easy access to wine and women and, if necessary, song, I have never participated in a social occasion where indiscriminate sexual activity took place. Or even highly selective sexual activity.

It is enough to make a person question his libido, not to mention his choice of bath soap. Or brood about his being clinically inhibited. A monk manqué. Going to hell without the send-off party.

Well, maybe it's not too late to give the sackcloth suit to the Salvation Army and put an ad in the newspaper personals: "Elderly gentleman seeks companionship of legal orgy. Party must be over by 8:00 p.m."

TALKING TURKEY

The visitor who ventures into Canada's newest West Coast nature preserve — the Gulf Islands National Park — may be excused for feeling that he or she has strayed into a branch of the Spanish Main. The names of some of the more significant islands — Galiano, Gabriola, Saturna — are redolent of the hot-blooded Spaniards whose ships penetrated the virgin strait dubbed Juan de Fuca.

Of these isles the most unspoiled in its saturnine temper — at least in the minds of us city types who own summer cottages there — is Saturna. *Caramba!* We'll spit in your eye and call it precipitation. We thumb our teeth at the U.S.A. into which our island juts below the belt of the forty-ninth parallel, daring the Americans to do something about it.

In the five-mile-wide Boundary Pass, a pod of orcas, aka killer whales, patrols the temperamental tides and discourages international regattas. The whales let off steam with an audible *whoomf* that sets the tone for debate among us on Saturna.

Agriculturally, Saturna is known only locally for its lush fields of cannabis — not native but happy to be introduced. (Even the mountains are high.) This heady grass thrives on a climate that excludes snow as an alien, probably smuggled in from the East.

The island's Mediterranean climate also favours the presence of a relatively mellow species of black widow spider whose bite is only mildly fatal.

All of this wildlife benefits from the fact that, on Saturna, hunting isn't allowed. Anywhere on the island. Nimrods have been a no-no for years. One result: the celebrated wild goats of lofty Mount Warburton Pike were never more feral. Nobody remembers the last time the primordial herd was sighted, but we all know that the wild goats are up there, somewhere, poised to butt the hell out of anything that moves.

Saturna's multitude of deer? Blatantly frivolous. The woods are merry with their giggles as they watch another fuming truck gardener install a new fence presumed to be high enough to thwart a deer's leaping in for lunch. On Saturna the buck doesn't stop here or anywhere else. He will peer into your parlour window and shake his head at your choice of TV entertainment.

However, for me, the most dramatic demonstration of the chutzpah of the island's wildlife occurs right on the curving coastal road to the lighthouse. Always at the same spot on an autobahn as little used as the Highway to Heaven. There I brake hard for the wild turkeys. In transit: the big tom and his harem of hens. In season: a gaggle of chicks.

Does Tom Turkey yield the right of way? In your dreams, stranger. The ordinary rooster may be chicken, but this turkey is *game*. He shows why Texans choose to hunt him: because he presents a challenge to humanoid dominance.

This turkey doesn't gobble. He talks *Turkey*. A tongue redolent of the ancient Turks who made raping and pillaging the national pastime.

He swaggers up to my car window so that we are eyeball to eyeball, wattle to wattle. The turkey doesn't say anything. His hen and chicks are exchanging rude remarks about my small, unmuscled coupe, but the boss is just silently challenging me to step out of the car. Which I would as lief do as confront a Chicago Bears linebacker.

I sense that this turkey views my car as a potential rival, sexwise. Its colour — red — is the same as that which predominates in the tom's spectacular array of hues. Which range from apoplectic crimson to quite peeved purple. Thus it is reasonable for me to conclude that this hostile cock, of a species not known for its intellect, is set to fight — to the death if necessary — with the farty foe of which I am the part that substitutes for a brain.

Being somewhat impetuous myself, I address His Turkeyship in a tone that is less than conciliatory.

"Eff off!" I suggest. Loudly enough to get a flutter out of some of his hens. But my suggestion is ill-received by their pasha. He just swaggers closer to my driver's seat door. Visions of door paint repair jobs dance through my head.

"Sir," I request hoarsely, "let me rephrase that. If you and your charming family proceed without further incident, I promise not to report this road obstruction to the Department of Highways."

Grudging. That is the disengagement this bullying turkey grants me. He shepherds his hens and chicks to his chosen ditch, but I sense no appreciation for their being spared the fate of roadkill.

Yet, despite my being delayed when I happen to be in a hurry to catch the ferry, I am vaguely disappointed those times when I *don't* come upon the roadblock of honkers. Has my gutsy Turk had a terminal tryst with a truck? Or have his hens got wind of women's lib, poultry division, and rerouted the commute?

Whatever, I slow down, anyhow, at that crossing spot. Because you never know when or where Saturna will suddenly express her Spanish *bravata*.

THE CALL OF THE WEIRD

Your phone rings. Ever alert to respond to any summons not issued by a court, or Marley's ghost, you answer the phone. And hear the voice that carols, "How are you?"

The voice isn't one you recognize as that of friend or family. But, ever appreciative of another's interest in your physical or mental condition, you say, "I'm fine, thanks. May I ask who is calling?"

"I represent Terminal Floor Cleaners. We happen to be working in your neighbourhood and can make you a special offer to —"

You hang up. You have been suckered by an apparently solicitous inquiry about your physical or mental condition. You are back to no one caring a damn about you, except maybe your dog. And even he has to be bribed with a bone.

However, you can feel much better if you've prepared a reply to the strictly commercial query, "How are you?"

For example: "Oh, thank God you called! I have this awful pain in my chest! *Urgh!* I've been trying to call 911, but someone keeps knocking the phone out of my hand! I think it's a family member, with a shopping bag over her head …"

Or in the middle of the evening while I am watching a tight hockey game, the phone call is from a realtor. "My apologies for calling this late," he pants, "but I have a buyer client who has fallen in love with your property. He has deep pockets. You can name your price."

"My property isn't up for sale." I hang up, vaguely discomfited by the need to be decisive without preparation.

The safest place to avoid phone calls is in your own home. The reason for this is that people prefer to phone you when they know you are busy — i.e., at the office, in the bathroom, or otherwise unlikely to prolong the conversation beyond the caller's time limit. Hence the supremacy of the cellphone. The only device the busy person will respond to live.

Walking on streets, riding in vehicles: this is where people are observed engaged in passionate intercourse with their cellmate. As I don't own a cellphone, I must resist the temptation to hover around my house phone. A watched kettle never boils, and a listened-for phone never rings.

Furthering the decline of the telephone as messenger is the tyranny of email. Which has largely eliminated the ear as a receiver. Now just a place to hang your glasses. The main disadvantage of using email rather than the phone is that the recipient may have been dead for several days, even weeks, before the sender learns why there has been a delay in someone's hitting the *reply* button.

This is why it is a good idea to phone our friends or relatives once in a while just to confirm they're not slumped over their computer, depressing the *delete* button.

Of course, the safest way to deal with unscheduled phone calls is to lift up the receiver and say nothing. Especially "Hello?" If the phone then yaps "Hello?" and the voice isn't familiar to you, or sounds commercial, give it the juicy raspberry and hang up. Unless you already have a mean streak. *Noblesse*, after all, *oblige*.

THE CORDLESS LOVER

Lovers used to make vows. Now they take precautions. Called for under the threat of VDT or, worse, reproduction other than Xerox. Better a safe than sorry, Romeo. People are too busy earning a living to make a career of being a Lothario.

Gone, Juliet's balcony. Romeo has to take the express elevator arriving too nauseated to remember her room number, let alone his rehearsed declaration of undying lust.

Today's career Juliet doesn't fuss daily with making her bed. Thus her Romeo is lucky if his seduction scene isn't a sofa, already occupied by a small dog with an attitude.

It also behooves him to hustle to an electronics store to check out the Talking Vibrator. The biggest advance in artificial stimulation since invention of the electric chair. Just inserting the batteries may suffice to produce blessed relief.

Too many would-be Romeos try to access a Juliet on the Internet, which proves to be an added hazard for the Juliet whose judgment depends heavily on how Romeo looks from behind.

Some young guys join a seniors' club believing that the women they meet there are too old to be rendered pregnant and seeking parental support payments. A perilous game, this, when young women are joining seniors' clubs to meet older guys with deep pockets.

Is it prudent then for a guy to join a seniors' club on the grounds that none of the lady members will be seeking a mate for her love boat? Answer: women never give up. They also make a distinction between love and sex. This is hard for guys to understand. But it is perilous to ignore the mindset.

Equally practical, many older women are taking judo classes whose programs are built around a kick in the crotch. For the guys, however, there are less painful ways of sterilizing Old Faithful.

Another venue for the raunchy retiree: the Alaskan cruise. Polar bears are now so tired of having wealthy Americans photographing their genital area that they refuse to mate without a lawyer.

Some worldly women have a repertoire of funny stories that they use on guys to measure both their sense of humour and their bladder's ability to retain contents. But it may not be smart to let a smile be your umbrella if it is raining.

As for guys who build a store of jokes with which to mollify a date and note any yellowing of her teeth: dirty pool. The gentleman's code has been abridged to a mild task. His date is less likely to have stars in her eyes than dollar signs. But the human drama needs players more than critics.

The most popular place to meet opposite-sexers today is the marathon run. Which provides the opportunity to wear revealing clothes in a benign setting. Women in particular relish a social milieu that favours flirting without the discomfort of high heels.

In summary, the most reliable female communication is the bottom line, i.e., the eloquent fanny. The delectable derrière. Ah, what sweet despair! To envy a pair of jeans!

THE CURSE OF PUNCTUALITY

Now that I am old enough to be quietly reflective, with some occasional snoring, it occurs to me that I have wasted a lot of my life by being too early for appointments. Sometimes minutes early, but more often hours, if not days.

I now envy folk who burble through life being tardy for every occasion but their own funeral. (I expect to leave for my own interment in plenty of time. It's a curse.)

Has this excess of punctuality earned me the respect of other people? *Au*, damn it, *contraire*. Being married to the clock is seen as a low form of wedlock.

When I was single, I would turn up for dates an hour early, having allowed time to be involved in a major accident and a subsequent delay in emergency.

Jeez, the hours I spent sitting in my car outside some girl's house, suspecting my watch of having stopped! I didn't trust the Swiss. All I knew was that being late for a date was a form of rudeness. No way to get a welcoming hug, let alone admission to that garden of delights, her kitchen.

Cool. That is how today's young people play it. Being late is cool. To be on time — or, worse, early — is uncool. Which is what I was, walking back and forth in front of a girl's residence, waiting for it to be time for me to make an even bigger fool of myself. (For her welcoming kiss, I would pucker up too soon, and often, like a goldfish on the make.)

Anyhow, now that my time, being abridged by aging, seems more valuable than when I was sitting in the car with a stopwatch in my hand instead of something more animate, one would expect that I could adapt to being stylishly late for things.

Not so. Oh, I may have knocked ten minutes off my earliness for a dentist's appointment, but medical staff still look at me as though I am some kind of masochist specializing in staring at old magazines.

Which, I insist, I am not. My problem is that, early in life, I modelled my schedules on that of Swiss trains. Running early.

I probably should consult a psychiatrist about my hyper-punctuality, but I sense that I would arrive far too early for the appointment. Probably set a new record for clinical prematurity.

I also avoid flying (on aircraft) because I know that I shall be at the airport far too early for my scheduled flight, my growth of beard attracting attention from security personnel.

My self-diagnosis of the cause of this premature appearance remains classified information. Instead I stick with the theory that nobody really admires the early bird that catches the worm. I identify with the worm.

Okay, I'll admit that a contributing factor may be that my own birth was premature. So I've been early for everything since.

Anyhow, at ninety, I now have only one appointment on my things-to-do pad. No way I plan to be early for *that* appointment.

God willing.

THE DILEMMA OF DISPOSAL

God knows, I *want* to be environment-friendly. Any time I happen to meet the environment — usually as a result of my going outside the house — I say, "Hi, En! How's it going with that pesky global warming?" Or "No problem, eh, with the so-called toxic waste?"

But I still feel guilty about my flawed relationship with a paintbrush. I know I should be using it as the appropriate means of transferring paint from the can to the fence. I can do the Tom Sawyer routine as well as any husband in the block.

What delays the operation is my apprehension about *cleaning* the paintbrush after I have got paint on it. The used brush doesn't qualify as garbage. Nor can it be recycled to produce wood and whiskers, carried by sewer to the nearest ocean. As for washing the brush under the tap, that would trigger the collapse of an ecosystem. (Tossing my used paintbrush in our local park's wading pool is an attractive option but would need to be done after dark when the park is subject to miscreants.)

If I clean my paintbrush with the garden hose, the worms may contract lead poisoning and the robins start laying acrylic eggs.

The bathroom toilet is inviting riddance, if I have painted with a small brush. But we recently had an explosion in our bathroom, the toilet violently regurgitating fifty years' worth of household detritus. What the city sewer crew charged me for relieving the constipation has discouraged me from any flushing other than my cheeks.

Nor does the city pick up used paint cans. Fussy, fussy, it insists that I transport my used paint can to a mortuary in a remote part of the city. Leery of driving my car on unfamiliar streets to this receptacle resting place, I have to take a taxi while carrying an empty paint can. Which can make a Yellow Cab nervous, if indeed it will pick me up at all.

But I don't need to have painted something in order to get into trouble. Frisking the postman for junk mail, for instance, might discourage him from delivering something I can't open without wincing.

I am glad that my city taxes pay for the recycling service to complement our garbage, but regret that the truckers are so picky about what they consider to be recyclable. If I put my old jockstrap in their blue box, surely they should be able to find someone who needs support.

As for the disposal of myself — inevitable despite the sentimental value — the decision has been made in favour of cremation. This should be more earth-friendly than grave-digging, which compromises both body and soil.

Meantime, there remains — and I use the word boldly — the problem of how to deal with my used paintbrush. I could, I suppose, ask to have it buried with me. Held in my hand as a token of Western civilization. But I hesitate to initiate a burial rite that compares so unfavourably with what archaeologists have found in Egypt's Valley of the Kings.

THE DREADED DIGITAL

O
f the several advantages of dying young, the most trenchant for a guy is: he avoids the digital examination of his prostate. The paradiddle.

This outrage usually occurs in the doctor's examining room, whose walls have been padded to muffle the scream of the patient. Who is a mature male learning why having the regular medical checkup enhances the option of his joining a Tibetan monastery.

Kids, in contrast, have no concern about the prostate gland. Girls, in particular, benefit from not having one. They are not the seeded players in the game of sexual intercourse.

So, it is only guys — usually the older guys — who are subjected to the humiliating probe. Which is the best reason for having a female physician: smaller hands. Less finger. The dreaded middle. True, she may be less likely to detect a prostate glitch, but the experience may not launch the patient into space, and an orbit of the half-astral.

However, some guys would sooner risk death than get a rectal exam from *anyone*. Unless heavily sedated by a pre-op at the pub. And no matter how many times a guy suffers this ultimate intrusion on his ass, or how violent that sexual assault may be, he must stifle any whimper or wail that betrays the manly mien he wants to maintain while lying on his face.

Our public health system has compromised the stiff upper lip by removing the financial excuse for not going to the doctor. Our wallet has betrayed our tush. Guys have lost the incentive to die young.

For our grandfathers there was a degree of heroism, even panache, in their ignoring any reproductive organ not front and centre. But now terror may be struck into the heart of any guy who finds that his old family doctor has been replaced by a *locum*, a burly young fellow with fingers like frankfurters, or Frankenstein.

True, there is no clinical evidence that getting a rectal exam can cause a guy's voice to change to alto. The legend that his testes will shrink to pebbles has no basis in medical records, though it isn't uncommon for his pubic hair to turn white or lose its curl.

"Just close your eyes," says one adviser, "and think of the rectal exam as the Good Fairy popping her wand into your grotto." Nice try, Doc, but euphemism fails to hack it in this case.

Let's face it: the rectal is a quick, cheap way for a doctor to check a man's prostate for lumps. The hand is quicker than the eye, let alone the MRI. But the effect may affect the way the guy walks. His mincing steps could attract the very people whom his privates need to avoid.

Which is why the Boy Scouts program should include instruction in the difference between a prostrate exam and a prostate exam, for which he is prone. It will be a lot more relevant when the kid gets older and has that first rectal exam that puts into question his being the noblest work of God.

THE DRUMMER BOY

One of my minor regrets as I lurch toward the sepulcher is that I failed to pursue my career as a percussionist. Yes, me the drummer in the family combo completed by my mother on piano. I can still hear the polite applause accorded to this nine-year-old and my accompanist by the meeting members of the Nelson, British Columbia, Rotary Club, whose rotation was lubricated by alcoholic beverage.

What a rush! For a kid whose peer group consisted of his pet rabbit! Today I realize that the accolade won by our concert owed a lot to the fact that my mother was a very attractive woman who graced the fashionable short skirts and high heels of that 1920s era. When she took a bow, I shared the tribute as if I were relevant. We all have our sources of self-esteem.

Yet I never took drumming lessons. If indeed such have been available, then or now. Drumming was something you picked up on your own, like measles. I feel sorry for today's kids who lean so heavily on the Internet for relief from tension.

Even more worthy of sympathy are those kids having to take violins lessons. There has to be a more than evident relationship between violin and violence. True, symphony orchestras batten on fiddlers while hiring but one percussionist. But who notices a cellist? He is lucky if he even gets to sit down. Whereas the player's sitting, as I dreamt of doing, amid a full set of drums makes him the resonant kin of Thor.

Does a drummer need to be slightly mad? Probably. As I recall some of my other activities as a kid — most of them involving firearms of varying degrees of lethality — I would say that society got off lightly from my drumming.

And before he lets himself be captivated by the vision of his leading a street parade, setting the tempo for a battalion of guys armed with nothing but guns, the drums candidate should understand that playing the drums is not only addictive but likely to restrict his residential accommodation to a tree house. Located some distance from civilization.

If the drums addict is renting his accommodation, he may find this hard to keep unless he has smuggled his tympani into the boarding house and lines the rooms with sound-absorbing carpet while giving his name as Ali Booboo.

Eric Nicol

THE GENESIS OF ME

So far as I know I wasn't born in a manger. An ordinary barn, yes. That would explain my subsequent hay fever. But I think my parents would have mentioned it if my nativity had drawn a crowd.

Certainly, in succeeding years, I was more of a repellant than an attraction. Thanks not to a manger but to mange. Rampant eczema. Even dogs seemed to avoid me. On the street, mothers steered their kids around me. Short pants, being the boys' garb of the time, I was glad to get my legs under my school desk. My teacher thought I was just studious.

The truth was that I felt leprous. A junior Lazarus. Career opportunity: begging in front of liquor stores.

Early on, my mother took me to a dermatologist. He wouldn't touch me. Literally. He examined me from behind his desk. Making no effort to hide his revulsion, he assured my mother that my eczema wasn't contagious. She didn't need to have the house fumigated. So long as nobody would touch me, the chances of my producing a nationwide plague were minimal.

Thus reassured, I was able to accept my low self-esteem with some allowance for always smelling of ointment. Even dogs avoided me. I wore gloves to school, winter and summer. Would have killed for long pants.

I avoided girls, lest their initial scream attract the attention of school authorities.

Eventually, I grew out of the eczema, but never gained the self-confidence needed for any kind of public life that involved being seen. Instead I became a writer. A solitary occupation, with no need to be physically attractive. Or smartly dressed. Slobville, in fact. I can write in my nightshirt, though I tend to drift off before the pencil gets the lead out.

Thus I have never been comfortable in the company of more than one person at a time, tops. Preferably the same person, as I have such trouble remembering names that have never run for public office. Anti-social ego. The worst kind.

I am most comfortable in a one-on-one relationship. With my wife or God, though I haven't heard from Him for a while. I believe that every writer should have a spouse or significant other as a contact with reality. It is very easy to become convinced that the reason why one's work is being ignored by critics is that they are all consumed by jealousy. Dogs in the manger of our God-given talent.

To be honest, the main benefit from being a social person is that of being able to talk and hold a drink at the same time. I have never mastered this trick. I either spill the drink or spill the beans, gossip-wise.

I wish that people would see these social failings as those of a rough diamond. But I suspect I'm more of an uncut clot.

Anyhow, I have reached the age when most people think that I am dead. "Oh," they ask, "are you still alive?" This is why I have regular medical checkups. I trust that my doctor would have told me if my zits had proved terminal.

THE JOY OF CREATIVE WRITING

The great appeal of creative writing is that it is something you can do in bed. Something else. Besides sleeping or whatever, that is.

Also, words are cheap. I find that I can construct an entire sentence for pennies a day. Any school dictionary will supply basic words. The rest can be picked up from studying graffiti on Gastown walls.

Also, for the writer, the cost of wardrobe is minimal. I myself am evidence that it is possible to lead a full creative life without ever getting dressed. Thus it wasn't until my son got married recently that I had to renew my acquaintance with a necktie. My Adam's apple went into shock. I had to leave the reception early, because my loafers were threatening to make a scene.

Now what should a writer *wear* to work if he or she is working at home? Clothes would make a good start if your furnace isn't working. I myself often write in my nightshirt. This saves time — no zipping, knotting, etc. — before retiring.

Next, *when* is the best time to write creatively? Morning, noon, or night? Answer: yes! You write when the spirit moves you. If the spirit doesn't get up off its ass, you can't really be blamed for just staring into space. However, too *much* spirit, from a bottle or flask, can cost you a whole sonnet. I myself have never been a heavy drinker, weighing one hundred and seventy, tops.

Now, having put it off as long as possible, *where* are you going to write? The professional writer, like me, probably has an office of his own. In the basement. With other preserved fruit.

I myself have creatively written in all sorts of circumstance. The Paris subway. A Sri Lankan jitney. A New York hotel. A garret, I don't recommend. Sounds romantic, but the steps can kill you. Literally. Or at very least restrict your intake of alcoholic beverage.

To sum up: nearly everyone over sixty has the urge to write a novel based on his life but with the masturbation bits edited out. This impulse shouldn't be suppressed unless you have good reason to believe there is something else you can do that won't harm the environment.

The main thing is not to develop resentment because publishers haven't even done you the courtesy of a printed rejection. Stop thinking about the *Times Literary Supplement* and work toward space in your neighbourhood newsletter.

Finally, keep in mind: having your book on your bookshelf means little if yours is the only bookshelf your book is on.

THE LAW OF PROBABILITY

If in the bathroom on business you drop the cap off a tube of medication onto the floor, what are the chances that the cap will roll into the heating grille and be gone forever? Check one:

1. minimal
2. 20–50%
3. 100% (i.e., inevitable)

Yes, number 3 is correct. If you had recognized this fact of physics before bending in the doomed attempt to intercept the cap, you might have avoided the forehead abrasion suffered in your collision with the sink. But probably not. You are obeying the law of inevitability. The idiot cousin of probability.

Scenario 2: You have been standing for hours in the queue of people waiting to buy a ticket to the major entertainment event of the season. What are the chances that when you finally reach the head of the lineup, an usher will come forth bearing the sign: SORRY FULL HOUSE.

Answer (of course): 100 percent.

Scenario 3: You are sitting at your desk, waiting for an important phone call from a client, a lover, or both. When the phone finally rings, what are the chances the call is from:

1. your mother-in-law

2.   someone getting a wrong number
3.   a phone company lineman up a pole

Answer (again): 100 percent each.

Some people try to modify the ill effect of the Law of Probability by staying in one place as long as they can without hearing the call of nature become a bellow ("yoo-hoo, doo-doo"). Even the most dedicated fatalist severely tests his phlegm when he steps into a public toilet. Where his zeal in averting his gaze from everything but feet below cubicle doors results in bodily collisions not covered by insurance.

Any naturally wary person will assume that his taking the bus will seat him beside a runny-nosed kid exhaling virus in volume. So instead he walks to work and gets hit *by the same bus that would have let him off with just a cold.*

Some people have tried to avoid the Law of Probability by going into politics and living in Ottawa or Washington. It didn't work.

The only way to thwart the gods that dictate the probable is to show no surprise when something comes at you out of left field. For all but a lucky few of us, left field is where the game of life is lost or won.

Que sera, sera, counsels the popular song, expressing an admirable resignation to the fact that the road of life is 90 percent pothole. Yes, this philosophy does smack of fatalism. No matter how many times his toothpaste cap falls down the bathroom heating grille, a person must retain his faith in the stock market.

Expecting the worst to happen is a brand of fatalism, a shrugging of the shoulder instead of leaning into the fickle wind of fortune. This is why the Buddha is seen sitting securely cross-legged and lost in a trance that thwarts probability. His mien is a model we may all usefully emulate. Provided of course that we have room service.

THE PRE-SHRUNK VIOLET

No, I do not see myself as the noblest work of God. Even if I've shaved. And have remembered to zip my fly. Instead I prefer to think of myself as a work in progress. Rather than the apotheosis of human evolution.

True, I do take quiet pride in my humility. If I didn't have a bad back, I would do more bowing and scraping. My wardrobe doesn't run to sackcloth and ashes. But I am on my knees a lot, praying for relief from humbleness.

I believe that I have the rumpled look that is *de rigueur* for any author who doesn't smoke a pipe. (Female authors are under even more pressure to look dowdy. A poetess in stiletto heels is an anomaly, scary even to imagine.)

I am keenly aware of the need to avoid *false modesty*. Which, like false teeth, can make you talk funny.

I strive for *empathy*, putting myself in another person's shoes regardless of his poor taste in socks.

Perhaps because I have never lived in the U.S. Bible Belt, I have no quarrel with Charles Darwin. But my trousers lost their crease during the last economic depression when I was nine. I accept that evolution has swung me out of the trees, scratching out a living. At the zoo I avoid eye-to-eye contact with a monkey, lest she — or, worse, he — become sexually aroused. It hasn't happened yet, but just once could be enough to get my name into *National Geographic*.

I remain aware that there is a very fine line between self-assurance (good) and cockiness (bad). My humility still needs work, I know. I have difficulty being consciously humble. Maybe I've been fawned on by too many headwaiters. Whatever, I have always had a flair for involving myself in episodes guaranteed to deflate my ego.

Yet I have avoided becoming a devout determinist. If you blame everything that happens to you on Fate, sooner or later Fate will get fed up and either hire a lawyer or, more likely, direct your path to an open manhole.

My morals also benefited from the fact that, in that early twentieth-century age of innocence, I didn't understand how girls worked. I had heard that a girl could become pregnant if she didn't take the proper precautions, but I had no idea what the proper precautions were. As for the *improper* precautions, such as her gelding her partner, these are, to me, a mystery wrapped, as the poet said, in an enigma.

However, I believe that I have recovered from being *a closet egotist*. That is, a person who goes into a closet to shout, "I am the greatest!" Doing this made my hanging pants shrink, I found, around the waist, and some of the neckties seemed to coil and hiss at me.

Aside from headwaiters, very few people treat me as a god. Even a *minor* deity would be nice. But the fact is they are too preoccupied with lesser matters — their job, global warming, etc. — or simply too arthritic to curtsy.

This is why I advise young career seekers to consider entering the priesthood. The money is better and you get to wear a dress (easy to wash).

The bottom line: be content with what you are, but be open to other offers.

THE SIMPLER

There is a market, I believe, for a Canadian-made automobile called the Simpler. The Simpler doesn't have all the bells and whistles associated with cars deriving from Detroit. It may *cluck* reprovingly, but is generally designed to reduce road rage to a snit or minor miff.

The Simpler is built for basic locomotion at a speed that eliminates the temptation to pass another vehicle unless that vehicle isn't in motion. The driver has the added peace of mind that comes with knowing that the Simpler will never exceed the speed limit unless descending a steep hill in the throes of brake failure.

The Simpler is a dream to park, having a natural tendency to avoid the road.

In regard to colour, the Simpler comes in several shades of black. It also goes black. The ideal car for people who join a lot of funeral cortèges just to get respect.

The Simpler should appeal to automotive masochists. The heating system consists of a Hudson's Bay blanket. And/or a hot-blooded blonde in the passenger seat. Which also strengthens the need to buy car insurance — the main financial burden for the Simpler owner.

In deference to Canadian road conditions — snow, ice, small children — the Simpler engine is an adaptation of the dishwasher. It is willing to sacrifice power to cleanliness. "The Immaculate Contraption" is just one of the praises heaped upon the Simpler in paid ads.

For safe driving the Simpler has all the bells and whistles — in lieu of brakes. By muting the horn, the Simpler automatically eliminates provocation unless the car is moving or parked without due discretion. In short, the Simpler doesn't beep. Instead, the manual includes the names of psychiatrists to whom the Simpler owner may take the vehicle for analysis if maladjustment is suspected.

In other respects the Simpler horn is a triumph of Canadian engineering, being muted enough to attract attention without sounding aggressive. On the negative side, the Simpler horn has been found to attract moose. Which is why the test ground was moved from Ontario to Florida.

The Simpler plant is surrounded by a high-security fence to prevent Chinese industrial spies from picking up ideas for a new generation of rickshaws. The fence will be electrified as soon as the company can find an electrical engineer to pedal the bike and generate power.

The Simpler is, of course, an off-road vehicle. This car actually *hates* highways. It can smell blacktop from miles away, rearing up on its hind wheels and snorting in a spirited fashion not usually found in a Canadian product other than skates.

As its contribution to population control, the Simpler has no back seat. Reason: research has shown that 80 percent of unwanted pregnancies may be traced to activity in the rear seats of conventional autos.

The front seat of the Simpler doubles as a prophylactic, being dominated by a steering wheel that gouges any activity involving a clutch other than that on the floor.

The Simpler is equipped with tires — one on each wheel — especially designed to grip on snow or ice. On a dry highway they tend to catch fire. But later models will have a complete sprinkler system fed by puddles.

Expected to be priced at about $100,000 for the basic model (no roof, but a plush monkey in the rear window), the Simpler is the ultimate uncovered wagon.

THE SOURCING OF A SKEPTIC

My qualifying as a bona fide, if not actually paranoid, skeptic dates from the dark day when my parents confirmed that, yes, there was no Santa Claus.

Since I was in high school at the time, the shock was doubly severe. Having enjoyed a rewarding relationship with Father Christmas for many years, only to have my faith shattered by people I had come to trust, I was doomed to spend the rest of my life doubting the existence of just about everything, including myself. (Maybe I'm just an idea in the mind of God.)

My parents' terminating Santa was especially traumatic for me, as I had only recently gone on record as having heard his sleigh's reindeer clattering to a stop on our roof. To this day I can still hear those happy hooves. And I am ready to argue that there can be no other explanation for the phenomenon, since my parents had no history of tap dancing in the attic. At least not after bedtime.

The point is that, for me intellectually, it was a straight line from my parents' putting paid to Santa — and with him a bunch of hard-working elves vital to the economy of the North Pole — to my embracing Bertrand Russell.

Into the vacuum created by the vapourization of the ample figure in the red suit has rushed a gaggle of other potential distributors of goodies: the NDP, the Swiss lottery, etc., none proving as reliable as Santa had been.

What prompted my parents to total Kris Kringle was the Great Depression. Which adversely affected his inventory of toys and slowed his sleigh down to a crawl to conserve ho-ho. The department store Santa had to wear padding to plump him up, and his bony knee was no treat to be sat on.

To complement that period of darkness, my teen years were conditioned by my assumption that babies were born via the navel. (I lacked the sex education provided by late-night television. Radio said nothing about the mechanics of human parturition.)

But how did an eight-pound baby manage to exit through an aperture second cousin to a keyhole? What was Mother Nature thinking when she made the natal escape hatch so pokey? No wonder some of the girls at our high school had to leave town to have their babies. The navel manoeuvre was too tortuous for the family to bear.

The mental vacuum created by the loss of Santa and the absence of sex education made my adolescent mind prone to fantasies, mostly about girls, later about determinism. Some of these still survive, though somewhat mellowed by time. And much as I appreciate the gifts of modern science, they have never quite compensated for my loss of the Easter Bunny.

THE VANISHING PIN-UP

I joined the Royal Canadian Air Force in 1942 as a potential fighter pilot. But the air force soon discovered there was no type of training craft in which I wouldn't become violently airsick. Sometimes before the plane even left the ground. I emetically bombed most parts of Alberta and an already disadvantaged Saskatchewan.

I was hastily distanced from aircraft and seconded, if not thirded, to the staff of *WINGS*, the air force monthly magazine. The magazine was loaded with an explosive full-page photo of a Hollywood glamour girl. The studios supplied us with glossy prints that added a new dimension to military breastwork.

Thus it came to pass in a grubby Ottawa office that one of my critical assignments — shared by the editor, the janitor, and anyone passing through — was to select each issue's pin-up photo A dicey assignment, but somebody had to tackle it. The photo, I knew, was a vital factor in sustaining the morale of thousands of airmen too busy fighting to create sexual fantasies without our ground support.

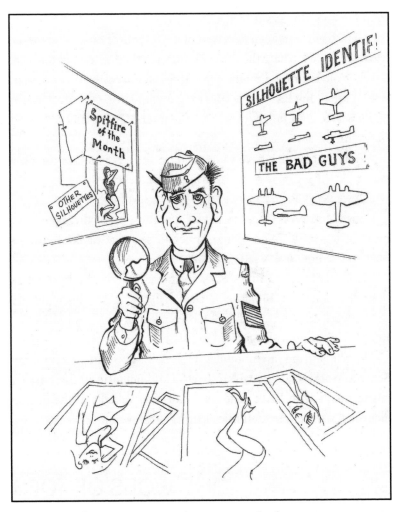

A crucial assignment, yes, but *someone* had to step up, or more likely sit down, and make a judgment between glossy eight-by-ten photos of the bounteous Jane Russell or Rita Hayworth in a swimsuit that could cause a tsunami or grabable Betty Grable.

Today the pin-up is kaput. The victim of Real Women? How could such a societal institution — the basis of the fantasies for millions of heterosexual guys — be relegated to a few glossy magazines never found in an airman's survival kit?

Thus have men been deprived of a vital source of sexual fantasy. Most are forced to base their dreams on what they observe at the local beach. Not, as a rule, a pretty sight. Thus, all too easily, Western man may relegate his lust to the overweight standards of those Eastern lands whose guys judge women by the pound. Pictorially restricted to fat shrouded in a tent.

Today a guy may have to depend on the strip joint as the only venue of titillation. An environment that degrades the awe with which we vets beheld the images of Betty and Rita.

The demise of the pin-up girl doubtless suits the agenda of militant feminists. Who would prefer to see men hankering for a hulk whose first love is saturated fat.

Result: more and more guys are forced to use the Internet as their sole source of titillation. I personally have not descended to those depths. (I suspect that Internet users are monitored by the RCMP, preparing a file of closet rapists.)

When sorting memorabilia I sometimes stumble upon my Second World War medals and relive momentarily those stirring engagements with Betty, Jane, and Rita. The Valhalla of the pin-up girl. Shall we ever see their like again? Probably not.

THE WOES OF TOES

It is not generally known, but old toe-nails, and especially old *big* toenails, are the hardest substance on Earth.

In comparison the diamond is putty. Tempered steel: no big deal. I can easily believe that South African natives use big toenail parings to cut diamonds. (A fact kept secret because common knowledge could affect the sale of engagement rings worldwide and thus encourage sexual promiscuity. Which, of course, doesn't need any encouragement.)

Another rarely discussed fact: no senior should attempt to cut a big toenail single-handed. Roughly 50 percent of 911 calls are from oldsters who pranged their backs in the course of the struggle to cut a big toenail.

My wife, who isn't given to extravagance, has her toenails cut by a podiatrist. This pruning may be okay for a woman (which my wife is), but for a guy it smacks of a decadent society. The jihadists would strike before I even had time to get my socks back on.

So I cut my toenails myself. This would be more feasible if my feet weren't at the end of my legs. Which aren't long, for my age, but seem to extend when I pick up the scissors. Thus my toes become inaccessible without a contortion that promises an interlude in emergency.

This is why I organize my toenail-cutting operation into three (minimum) stages, all within crawling distance of a telephone. Then I muster the material needed for the assault:

1. Spectacles designed to stay clamped on the head despite violent shaking. *Not* your reading glasses. Your toenail is without literary value. Wear shatterproof glasses or a coalminer's goggles. If you can avail yourself of a friend or relative to hold a magnifying glass while you cut your old toenail, jolly good!

2. Surgery arc lights. Hospital emergencies are crowded with seniors who have tried to cut their toenails by ordinary bed lamp. (Sunlight is okay if the sky is *totally* clear of clouds. Which can reduce five digits to four in the twitch of an eye.)

3. Nail-cutting shears. Ordinary scissors are useless for cutting old toenails. *And* you can sprain a thumb in the course of the struggle. Safer to use than any scissors is the nail *file* or rasp.

But this tool also requires accessing the feet for a longer period of time than is compatible with ever straightening the leg again in your lifetime.

This is why Chinese Mandarins never cut their nails on toes or fingers. Thus manifesting their not having to do work. Or wear socks. On which our Western toenails wreak a terrible toll. Some of us will swear that we can actually *hear* our big toe sawing an exit from a valued argyle sock that may have sentimental value as a wedding present.

It's no holes barred. This is why, despite the pain involved, some seniors actually *remove* their socks from their feet — especially when sleeping in a strange bed — and let that ravaging big-toenail wreak its havoc on someone else's sheets.

There can be no doubt that the horny brute works in collaboration with New Zealand sheep farmers — *Baaaaa!*

TITILLATING IT AIN'T

True, the science of human anatomy has come a long way. But it still hasn't answered — to *my* satisfaction at least — the vital question: Why do guys have nipples?

Being a guy myself, I find this mystery to be particularly relevant. I know what most of my other body parts are for, even though some of them work only part-time. But this pectoral feature, tits, seems to be quite supernumerary.

If I were a female, I could see the point. (*Two* points, actually, but I digress.) But I do not, to my knowledge, produce milk. Not even

1 percent. Never have, I believe. My relationship with infants has always been at arm's length or farther. Suckling is, I understand, one of the joys of motherhood, but even as a father of three reproductive accidents, I never felt that my bosom was a wasteland.

I am old enough to remember a time when even prizefighters wore vests, and all men topped their bathing suits at the beach. Then somebody asked why, I guess, and men started going topless, drawing additional attention to their boobs.

Not me. I never learned to swim, thus preserving my modesty for the proper environment of the marital home. True, my not having a hairy chest may have contributed to my fear of being seen as effeminate — and getting hit on by near-sighted letches.

All of which has doubtless contributed to my having a poor attitude toward my nipples. I haven't even looked at them for years, as I assume they continue to enjoy their status of being utterly superfluous.

How could this happen, this booby-hatching? My guess is that at some point in the evolution of homo sap our ancestral ape man shared the baby nursing duties with the female until he realized it was time to get out of the tree and into a fight with a mastodon — i.e., evolution.

Or maybe we should take a hard look at Adam and Eve. Scripture fails to mention whether Adam was created with nipples. But in all pictorial representations he is accessorized with the lactiferous.

One has to wonder: Did the Creator originally plan to make man/woman as an all-purpose being with the same pectoral accessories? The question remains strangely moot. Checking with another revered authority, the *Oxford Dictionary*, we find the definition of *nipple*: "… a short section of pipe with a screw thread at each end for coupling." The sexual connotation is obvious.

Yet no woman has ever said to me, "I really dig your dugs." If the nipples are supposed to be a factor in coupling, I have wasted a lot of money on undershirts.

Okay, as one of life's mysteries, men's nipples are minor league. But then I never did make it to the majors.

VIRGIN ON SILLY

For most of my youth, my sex life was on hold. I would sooner have held a girl, but I wasn't sure why. Thus I remained a virgin for so long I was afraid I would start attracting pilgrims. Good Saint Nicol. Ho-ho, humbug.

Aiding and abetting my chastity was my ignorance about the mechanics of sexual intercourse. My parents never discussed the matter with me, as if begetting me had made the whole subject painful for them. My father, in particular, looked upon me as a source of questions he didn't want to answer. Such was pioneer life before the Internet.

For me, puberty meant becoming apprehensive around girls. I didn't know how they worked. They didn't come with instructions, like my Meccano set.

As a teenager, I became aware that one part of my body seemed to have a mind of its own. I had to screen my thoughts for provocative material, of which I seemed to have an unlimited supply. Not knowing a hormone from a trombone, I feared I was interning as a sex fiend.

My parents failed to enlighten me about sex probably because I reminded them of one of the hazards.

Because my parents didn't subscribe to any orthodox religion, I never went to church summer camp, the main source of sex education at that time. Some of my friends learned how to have sex in a canoe. I didn't even learn to swim.

As a further deterrent to normal relations, my guardian angel gifted me with eczema. Which really loved the wool bathing suit prevalent in my youth. I suspected that if I went to summer camp I would be put in a hut by myself. With a skull-and-crossbones sign on the door.

As for erotic stimulation, I depended entirely on our local private lending library. To which I biked every Saturday afternoon, to browse among the adult novels whose graphic sex scenes, though mild by today's standards, got me more aroused than one would expect from fairly small print. The elderly couple who owned the library tolerated my using their premises as an aphrodisiac. And I certainly expanded my vocabulary, among other things.

I didn't attend my high school graduation dance because that would involve grasping a girl around the waist and getting expelled for indecent enclosure. Matriculating in public.

Because of these sexual inhibitions, I never reached the age of consent. I went straight from the age of repression to the age of wha hoppen?

Colouring my response to puberty was the circumstance of my mother being a very shapely woman who wore spike heels to go to the butcher shop. We ate prime beef at our house, but the price I paid was in ignoring girls clad in sensible shoes.

I don't remember where or when I lost my virginity. I still feel that I just mislaid it. One day it will turn up, making my three adult children look pretty silly.

Meantime, my advice to kids: don't be in a hurry to become an adult. It involves getting *older*. Who needs it?

WHEN ANTIQUITY GETS PERSONAL

At age ninety I am finding that my sex life is diminished. Hell, I'm lucky if I can mount stairs. I don't lust like I used to. For chocolate bars, yes. But unwrapping something with legs would be a challenge I prefer to avoid.

No one sees me, I believe, as an old goat. An old ass, maybe, but nothing lascivious. A very minor compensation, this, for being prehistoric.

Taking my cue from winemaking, I believe that much depends on lying horizontal, corked, for an extended period.

When I was younger, I was quite willing to provide an escort service, if you were going to hell. No more. My special taxi fare for seniors doesn't cover perdition.

On the plus side, my conscience is no longer plagued by the teenage sin of emission … nocturnal. Waking up in a puddle of my own making, not to be blamed on the bladder, made me neurotic about my entire sub-equatorial region.

Yes, I should now be grateful for not having to wear a diaper. But I'm not. Second childhood be damned!

"Time to stop and smell the apple blossoms," they say. Well, I did smell an apple blossom once, and got a bee up my nose. There was probably a message there that I missed.

At ninety I am better informed about sex. Too late, of course. On the other hand, a little knowledge can be a dangerous thing if it gets into your drawers. (You may quote me on that. In fact, I'll be quite disappointed if you don't.)

I no longer need to worry about my financial status. But I do, anyway. It's a filthy lucre habit. The problem is I never recovered from the trauma of the Great Depression of the Dirty Thirties. I am thrifty about spending. Maybe not a tightwad, but my wad sure ain't loose.

I deny that when I open my wallet it creaks. It's my wrist. I had to remove the watch because it was telling time. Nobody had asked. Now I am timeless (my writing, I still have to work on).

Physically, my reflexes aren't as instantaneous as formerly. There may be a wait time between stimulus and response. I encourage my body to take a seat while my neurons decide whether action is feasible. I avoid loads, don't even carry a grudge.

When I hear the call of nature, however, I don't wait for an echo.

I have found that if you ignore pain, it will just get offended and hurt worse.

As for greed, mine is pretty much limited to my sleeping time. I can't seem to get enough of it. Dormantly insatiable. My ardent embrace is in the arms of Morpheus. Even though his breath isn't to die for.

WHIPPER SNAPPER

Seriously considering self-flagellation, are you? Tempted to purge your feeling of guilt by flogging the flesh that has got you into trouble?

Hold the quirt! You may be disappointed to find how difficult it is to scourge the flesh without hurting yourself. And *accidental* scourging doesn't count as purgation. Also, if you get blood on the carpet your partner may deal you a slap that has no spiritual value whatever.

Another deterrent: whips aren't cheap to buy. Good quality leather will cost you an arm and a leg. And you don't want to be seen browsing in a saddlery shop by friends or family who know you don't own a horse.

Maybe you should ponder just *why* hating yourself in the morning has spread into the evening, interfering with your normal excesses. So, check: what does Freud have to say about self-abuse? Answer: nobody knows. He may have said something after a few drinks, but it wasn't recorded.

So it is up to the individual — you and me, but especially you — to be on the alert for symptoms, none of which are clearly defined but may include pulling out your ear hair by the roots. If caught in time, hating yourself may be reduced to minor loathing.

What about tearing up your birth certificate in an attempt to convince yourself you are too young to know better? Answer: futile. There is always someone out there who has known you long enough to know that sucking a pacifier is inappropriate.

The main drawback to detesting yourself is that it is a rather lonely activity. There may be a lonely hearts club out there, but masochists are, by and large, not joiners. And your own family may find excuses for not visiting you, except at Christmas When they will stay only long enough to last them until next Christmas.

Now, your family may urge you to see a psychiatrist. They will do this even though they know that most psychiatrists are severely maladjusted themselves and are seeing a psychiatrist also. They still reveal their condition by keeping their knees tightly crossed, like a virgin at a frat party.

So it is pretty much up to you to maintain a semblance of sanity unless assured of privacy. In this respect it is safer to use body language. Remember that your eyes are what blab mental confusion unless they are already crossed. And you can never go wrong in a group by just closing your eyes and practising a serene smile, one that never leaves your face even to go to the bathroom.

Think Buddha. Not sitting cross-legged, of course. (You may

be unable to get up without violent assistance, and there goes your priestly aplomb.) But you can't go wrong with maintaining a benign smile, regardless of all circumstances, except perhaps fire or flood.

The main thing is not to be carried away by a vogue for self-immolation. As sure as you're born, the moment you finally get the barbed wire wrapped around your genitals, it will be seen as cliché masochism. Stay cool, Buddha.

WHORE HOUSING

Our exemplary welfare society, which provides so generously for other seniors' housing, doesn't seem to include a retirement home for prostitutes. Not all of whom can find a place in Canadian politics.

This, surely, is shoddy treatment of ladies of the evening, whose calling spares untold numbers of "nice" girls a sexual assault that their freedom of movement and association would otherwise incite.

Yet we provide for the pasturing of persons found in the bawdy house we call Parliament. (From the French word *parler*, meaning audible issuance of hot air.) However, our Parliament has given talking a bad name. One unsuitable for text such as this, which may find its way into the school classroom. Suffice it to say that the operative word has the first syllable *bull*, then gets excretory.

Now it was once believed that if people were allowed to express their dissatisfaction with their government by means other than holding their nose, they would eventually rid themselves of *all* forms of government in a utopian state of anarchy. Why would so many men subject themselves to humiliation by the golf course except to escape tyranny by state, job, or spouse? The rough is relatively smooth.

I myself have never availed myself of the services of a prostitute. Not knowingly, anyhow. This despite a year-long residence in Paris where so many of its admirers have experienced the Eiffel Tower as not the only memorable erection.

Today temptation is much reduced, not only by my age but by inhabiting a middle-class neighbourhood where no one walks the streets except the postman. And he doesn't appeal to me.

However, it does seem that virtue depends highly on one's neighbourhood. For a time I lived in a boarding house area of London where morals were pliable. This did test my sturdy Canadian inhibitions, founded on the notion that that foreplay was a tennis doubles position. But I must have been on the wrong floor. Rectitude was rampant.

So I moved to a lodging in Knightsbridge where knighthood was no longer in flower, having been eroded by the kind of profligacy that now threatens Toronto. The boarding house taught me that it is bad policy to have separate sex with two women living in the same building. Unless the building is the Empire State.

I saw myself as a good egg waiting to get laid, but soon found that natural charm wasn't enough. Men are such romantics! It is women who have both feet on the ground. Just because they are wearing spike heels doesn't mean they are pushovers. A physics lesson that should be taught in high school at the latest.

It is argued that it is morally better to hire a whore than to despoil a virgin. This is a hard choice that can make a man hesitant to wink, even when he has grit in his eye. Fortunately, today there is less chance of a guy hitting on a virgin unless he is hanging around a kindergarten.

Anyhow, it seems a shame in our welfare society that there is no state-funded retirement home for old whores where they could buy drinks at a reduced price. But this is one crusade I am reluctant to embark on. A discretion endorsed by my wife.

WHOSE GLOBE IS IT, ANYHOW?

Okay, so global warming is going to desiccate the planet for future generations. Tough titty! Does anyone really believe that I am going to give up my gas-guzzling coupe, or replace my air conditioning with a windmill, just to provide a livable environment for people to whom I haven't even been introduced? Surely, you jest?

And what is this nonsense about deforestation being bad for trees? Defenestration, yes. I worry about being thrown out a window. Probably by a green activist. But forests and I have never been intimate. *One* tree, okay, I can relate to that. But if you get a whole lot of trees together, first thing you know, you've got *woods*. Which — and here I speak as a person often lost in one — can be a frightening type of vegetation.

I am also being urged to be concerned about the thousands of other species dying out every year because I am not riding a bicycle. Damn it, I do *not* use an electric toothbrush. My teeth are green. Saving juice.

Yes, yes, I can believe that thousands of other species are dying out every year. But none of them is man. Our species is more numerous than ever, as anyone knows who has to take the elevator to the office.

WHY PAIN HURTS

Those whom the gods love dies young.
— Menander, 342–292 B.C.

To prove his point, Menander died at fifty. His trenchant observation suggests that he probably had a back problem.

Today an aging population afflicted with back pain has made the fortune of the pharmacies that are second homes to seniors. We may have forgotten the names of family members, but we keep our pharmacists' names on the tips of our tongues. With backup tattoos on our wrists.

Some of us supplement our pharmacists with a faith in God and Aspirin. Prayer and Bayer. Leery of multi-syllable medical terms. (For years I thought an analgesic was a painkiller you put up your ass. My doctor once suggested I have a colonoscopy. "How about a semi-colonoscopy?" I countered, spraining our relationship.)

Thus encouraged to practise self-medication, I frequent the clinic formally known as the liquor store. Where I can purchase a therapeutic Australian wine without a prescription from my doctor. Alcohol kills germs, and they die happy. It may rough up my liver, the organ that produces bile, the disgusting source of bad temper. Good riddance!

However, wine as a palliative isn't indicated in certain situations such as operating a vehicle or cleaning a firearm. Hence the genesis of the most prevalent palliative of our time: *the pain patch.* I, personally, have done exhaustive research on the effectiveness of the pain patch and its relationship to premature aging. I have learned — at some expense to my nervous system — that applying the pain patch can put your blood pressure in orbit of the original problem. The safety rules:

1. Never attempt to apply a pain patch to any part of your body without the presence of another adult, preferably someone with training in panic suppression.
2. Remove the plastic sheath from the pain patch. This should never be done in the presence of children. Reason: the delicate operation requires not only a cunning fingernail but the steady hand of an eye surgeon. *No alcohol* consumption for twenty-four hours prior to applying the pain patch.
3. Discard the sticky sheath. This is impossible, of course, unless you are three-handed. Most pain-patch users park the sticky sheath on their forehead where it may remain unnoticed for weeks if they lead a sheltered life.
4. Apply the naked pain patch to whatever part of your anatomy hurts. Usually the back. The dorsal outback. The small of your back, which was never smaller. The manoeuvre requires exquisite timing. Indeed, the strongest argument for having a partner in life is to attend to your back long after your front stops whining.

To sum up: guys who have married a nurse have, statistically, a better chance of surviving their pain patch application. So long, of course, as she doesn't develop a drinking problem. Now about the news of a birth-control patch. Applied directly on a guy's fly …?

WIND WATCH

In regard to air quality, there are several dangerous emissions, but none more life-threatening than farting during your own wedding ceremony. I deny that I speak from experience. But I have attended other social occasions where atmospheric conditions suddenly worsened to accelerate departure of guests.

Not *my* fault, I insist. I wear a deodorant strong enough to take on any uninvited gust. If I am required to attend some event at which other people are present, I restrict my diet to grub even blander than usual. Before a driver's licence test, I may not eat at all. I have found that there is a fine line between being inoffensive and fainting from hunger.

The frivolous fart is one of the strongest reasons for the older person to have a house pet. A canary may be too small to be a plausible source of an ill wind. A dog is more culpable, especially a large dog like the Great Dane. But the feed bill may blow you away.

"That darn cat!" my elderly grandmother would exclaim. The feline learned to accept the libel. Even though it had been lying fast asleep at the time of the alleged crime.

The wayward wind may help to explain the enormous popularity of outdoor cafés in cities like Paris where the food is spicy and highly charged with potential to commit a major offence. As a student in that broad-minded metropolis, I still had difficulty accepting the fart as a compliment to the chef.

This reticence may be a Canadian trait. Strange, though, as we are blessed with the great outdoors. There have been one or two isolated cases of an outhouse being projected skyward. But we are better known for being withdrawn, rather than being effusive, at either end.

Now what about that relatively harmless effusion, the BURP? (Sorry about the capitals. Beans for lunch.) Okay, first we must distinguish between the burp and the belch. Belching is totally unacceptable unless one has clear evidence there is no other person, or sensitive wildlife, within the immediate area.

The burp, in contrast, is quite tolerable, socially, and may even help to break an awkward silence at a funeral.

Much more horrid is the *hiccup*. A spell of the hiccups can totally ruin a person's air of insouciance. It may terminate an opera contralto's career, if they take over the voice box during an aria. Though few in the audience would suspect a problem.

Bystanders always rush to the aid of a hiccupper, fearing damage to the environment. These measures include:

- slapping the face
- pounding the back
- punching the stomach

Any or all of these responses may aggravate the hiccups into a full-fledged vomit. This will cure the hiccups but create a painful cleanup bill. It is wiser to allow the hiccup attack to subside of its own accord, even though this may take hours, days, or quite tiresome weeks. Be prepared to change your vacation plans.

The safest workout is to exercise caution. In moderation, of course. A couple of hours a day should keep the ill wind down.

Old Is In
A Guide for Aging Boomers
978-1-55002-524-8
$16.99

Is impotence contagious? At what age should a senior be surgically separated from his automobile, or obligated to donate his sex toys to the Salvation Army? These and other timely questions are among those not answered in Eric Nicol's latest cure for serious reading. This palsied opus responds to demographics warning that our Western society is about to be engulfed by a tidal wave of seniors.

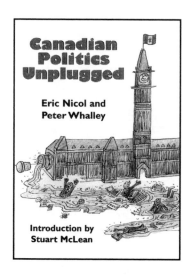

Canadian Politics Unplugged
with Peter Whalley
978-1-55002-466-1
$19.99

Canadian Politics Unplugged concentrates on the central problem of democracy in a country that is too big to digest without getting gas. Readers are assured that the authors have studied Canadian politics for years from a safe distance and enjoy the unique perspective of never having been elected to high office, low office, or any place where wearing shoes is mandatory.

Available at your favourite bookseller.

 **DUNDURN PRESS**
www.dundurn.com

What did you think of this book?
Visit www.dundurn.com for reviews, videos, updates, and more!